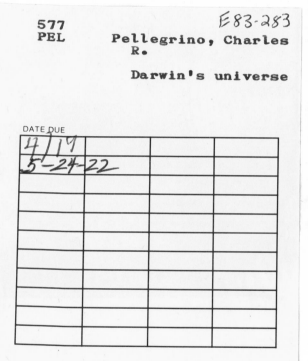

DARWIN'S UNIVERSE
Origins and Crises in the History of Life

DARWIN'S UNIVERSE
Origins and Crises in the History of Life

Charles R. Pellegrino
Jesse A. Stoff

 VAN NOSTRAND REINHOLD COMPANY
NEW YORK CINCINNATI TORONTO LONDON MELBOURNE

Manufactured in the United States of America

Published by Van Nostrand Reinhold Company Inc.
135 West 50th Street, New York, N.Y. 10020

Van Nostrand Reinhold Publishing
1410 Birchmount Road
Scarborough, Ontario M1P 2E7, Canada

Van Nostrand Reinhold
480 Latrobe Street
Melbourne, Victoria 3000, Australia

Van Nostrand Reinhold Company Limited
Molly Millars Lane
Wokingham, Berkshire, England

15 14 13 12 11 10 9 8 7 6 5 4 3 2 1

E83-283

Library of Congress Cataloging in Publication Data

Pellegrino, Charles R.
  Darwin's universe.

  Bibliography: p.
  Includes index.
  1. Cosmology. 2. Life—Origin. 3. Darwin, Charles,
1809-1882. I. Stoff, Jesse A. II. Title.
QB981.P44   1982   577   82-8352
 ISBN 0-442-27526-9   AACR2

To our parents, who took us to the American Museum-Hayden Planetarium and showed us boulders from the other side of the sky. And to all those at the Dorothy P. Flint 4-H camp where, for better or for worse, the seeds to this book were planted.

Foreword

A part of the child in all of us seems made to experience in a solitary way the touch of the universe. At one time or another who hasn't watched a bug crawl, or listened to the blood flux through moments of quiet, or felt a weight of time in the heft of a rock. Somehow the impersonal grandeur of the world impacts our consciousness and leaves on each its special mark. The mark can be one of fear, aloneness, awe, and insignificance mixed with a bravado of the opposites. This blend of wonders is our human condition and it's no surprise we view the condition with the fascination of a love-hate relationship.

Another part of that same inner human-child remains unfulfilled until the wonder and awareness of the world just felt is shouted to anyone who will listen!

Perhaps that's one reason why the question of origins has so attracted us at all creative levels of human endeavor. To approach that question is to become aware of the many faces of the Universe only to find even more fascinations beyond. Charles Pellegrino and Jesse Stoff's *Darwin's Universe* is the story of the origin of life (and its subsequent changes), which requires another story of the origin of the Earth, which requires yet another story of the origin of the Universe. . . . It is these stories within stories and plays as yet untold that are seemingly effortlessly fitted together as best as our sciences now know. This book is not a detailed compendium of the large literature on the topic;

rather it is a synthesis of these many specialities of contemporary science. It shows at once how much and how little we know—and how fresh and absorbing any of the sciences can be when applied to such a quest.

Clair E. Folsome,
Professor of Microbiology
University of Hawaii at Manoa

Preface

This book had its genesis in a friendship between two teenagers with common interests. I was then interested in fish, while Jesse occupied himself with meteorites. Jesse went on to medical school, while I took up zoology. Together we published articles in *Sky and Telescope* and *Astronomy;* and together we became pack rats. Today our bookshelves are a crazy-quilt work of papers from seemingly unrelated sources. Our offices and our homes are cluttered with fossil insects, glacial debris, meteorites, dinosaur bones, and assorted—er—artifacts. My attempts to explain to visitors what living and fossil crabs have to do with amber, climate, and dinosaurs, much less how they are connected to meteorites and Martian glaciers, have met, I think, with limited success. But they *are* connected. Viewed from a distance they are all part of a broader picture: a single image in which chemistry and biology converge with geology and astronomy. When we step back from our planet, looking at it as if it were another, we can see immediately that we are hitched to everything else in the universe. And we realize that we can never speak about ourselves or our origins without, at the same time, speaking about the other side of the sky.

Many colleagues have taken the time to provide helpful information, criticisms of individual chapters, encouragement, technical assistance in the laboratory, identification of specimens, et cetera. I am particularly indebted to Clair E. Folsome, Gerard R. Case, Richard M. Pearl, Edward I. Coher, August Schmitt, Alice Gray, Norman D. Newell, Niles Eldredge, Stephen Jay Gould, Luis Alvarez, Andrew J. Maslowski, Bartholomew Nagy, Harold C. Urey, John Wells, Bob Wear, Merv Loper, Ken Goldie, Mark Munro, Eric Stevens, John Whetren, John D. Collin, Jim W. Cole, Frank Andrews, Edward R. Harrison, William Kaufmann III, Carl Sagan, Don Peterson, Torrence V. Johnson, Joseph A. Wynecoop, Jurrie J. Van der Woude, Frank Bristo, and Eric Rosen (our editor). But, of course, none of the above are to be held accountable for any heresies that remain.

Special thanks are also due to Mrs. Dobie, Barbara and Dennis Harris, Agnes Saunders, Ed Mcgunnigle, Mr. and Mrs. John Pellegrino, and Tige, my wife, my right-hand man, my best friend.

Charles R. Pellegrino
Wellington, New Zealand

God does not play dice with the universe.
Albert Einstein

The study of life and its origins has always fascinated me. The more I have studied the more I have come to respect the intricacies of biochemical metabolism and the evolutionary mechanisms that lead to the miracle of life.

Scientists and philosophers have long debated the question of what brought about the monumental transition from inanimate matter to living organism. My own studies lead me to believe that there is an "energy principle" that is basic to life. This principle may be described in the following way: life, in essence, is the creative energy that orders the entropic patterns of matter in accordance with its own rhythmic processes. Living physiologic systems are not in (chemical) equilibrium but are maintained by these energies in a "steady-state," nonequilibrium metabolism. Thus, life does not appear to carry material forces on to a stronger manifestation of ther own inclination; on the contrary, life subdues and metamorphoses their inherent physical laws.

Conjectures about the origins and nature of life have largely centered about a reductionistic analysis of numerous prebiotic systems such as coacervates, critroens, proteinoid microspheres, et cetera. It is easy for one to become absorbed by the theoretical complexities of this primordial soup but, ultimately, one must not lose sight of the genius of the Master Chef.

Jesse A. Stoff
New York, New York

Contents

DARWIN'S UNIVERSE
Origins and Crises in the History of Life

1
Bang!

You ask me what God was doing before he created the materials of Heaven and Earth. He was creating Hell for people who asked questions like that.

Saint Augustine

Something hidden! Go and find it!

Rudyard Kipling

We live in a fascinatingly violent and beautiful universe. For thousands of years, human eyes have been looking at the sky and giving names and legends to its objects; for hundreds of years we have been using telescopes and finding newer, fainter objects. We have been comparing them against the older, more familiar ones, turning our imaginations loose, making up new stories to explain both the new and the old objects, and then designing experiments to test the stories.

As stay-at-home observers, looking outward from our solar system, we have discovered a universe that appears to be scattering to all points of the celestial compass, one that is blowing up, even as we watch it. It is as though the Milky Way and Andromeda and their neighbors were all caught up in the aftermath of a stupendous explosion. This observation, regarded by many cosmologists as one of the greatest discoveries of our century, is the crux of the new story of Genesis. Its first paragraphs were put to paper in 1845 by the Dutch meteorologist Christopher Heinrich Dietrich Buys-Ballot, who had a story to tell and had developed a splendid experiment with which to

1

drive his message home. He hired an orchestra of trumpeters and persuaded them to play a fanfare while standing on an open flatbed pulled by a locomotive hurtling through the countryside outside Utrecht. Buys-Ballot and his friends enjoyed the performance from a railroad platform beside the tracks and noticed, as he'd predicted they would, that the trumpets were higher-pitched when the train approached than when it raced away in the opposite direction.

What they had witnessed was a change in frequency as the train passed. Soundwaves from the approaching trumpeters were compressed to shorter wavelengths than usual, and the tones sounded higher to observers on the platform. As the train receded, the tones were stretched out to longer wavelengths than usual and appeared to drop in pitch. If you listen to the engines of a jet as it passes over your head you will notice the same phenomenon. It is called the Doppler effect and applies to light as well as sound. (It also provides an important example of the barrier between the observer and the observed: To the band leader racing along with Buys-Ballot's hired orchestra, or to a passenger on the jet, no distortion of pitch would be perceived.)

If a bright white star is traveling toward you at sufficient speed, its light will be compressed in front of it to waves of shorter length and will be distorted toward the blue end of the spectrum. Since blue light represents one of the shortest wavelengths of all the colors of the rainbow, this displacement of spectral lines toward shorter, bluer wavelengths is called *blueshift*. Conversely, if the star is speeding away from you, the wavelength of its photons (the massless particles, or "quanta," of which light, according to the *quantum theory,* is composed) will be stretched out behind it, resulting in a *redshift*. We are referring here to a shift of spectral lines—a kicking over to one side or the other—not to a visible change in the colors of stars. It is true that the sky is filled with blue and yellow and red stars, but these colors have essentially nothing to do with blueshifts and redshifts. Stars are red, white, or blue simply because they have different surface temperatures. Although light from a receding star is indeed shifted toward the red, the star's normally invisible light—the ultraviolet rays, X-rays, and gamma rays—will be carried along by the redshift into the blue part of the visible spectrum. Hence, no color change may be observed at all. What we do see, when we examine the spectrum of an out-racing star, is a shift of certain dark, prominent lines toward the red. (These lines arise from the absorpsion of light by specific elements within the atmosphere of a star and are normally found at well-defined positions along the spectrum.)

The extent of blueshift or redshift can be used as an indicator of how fast an object is moving toward or away from you. Using normal spectral lines as a guide, astronomers have discovered that, aside from stars in our own galaxy and a few close neighbors, all the galaxies and quasars in the universe seem to be rushing away from us at several thousand kilometers per second. (*Quasars,* or "quasi-stellar objects," are the most distant objects currently known. They are generally believed to be abnormal nuclei of very distant galaxies and are extraordinarily bright for their size).

And here we run up against a paradox. During the sixteenth and seventeenth centuries, men like Galileo Galilei challenged commonly held notions that the Earth was the center of the universe, and were subsequently asked many questions by the Vatican's Supreme Sacred Congregation of the Holy Office. Their "heresy" has since been accepted as fact (although there are still a few diehards who will tell you, among other things, that "every time those scientists send one of those rockets up to the moon it causes bad weather in Nebraska").

Now, astronomers tell us that all the contents of the heavens appear to be moving away from the Earth. But they only appear to be doing so because the same thing is happening everywhere. As near as we can tell, every galaxy is rushing away from every other galaxy, as though the universe were being inflated like a gigantic balloon. Each galaxy is a speck on the surface of that balloon; and as the balloon expands, each speck sees its neighbors moving away from it, perceiving itself as the *center* of the expansion. But, in truth, there is no center of the universe—no edge, either—anymore than there is a precise, central point on the surface of a balloon.

If we imagine the expanding universe as an inflating rubber balloon, we must bear in mind that the galaxies are not hurtling away in all directions through space, but are actually at rest, like specks on a balloon, in space that is expanding. We should also try to remember that our expanding balloon analogy represents our three-dimensional space compressed into two spatial dimensions on the surface of the balloon. The radial direction of the balloon is not a fourth spatial dimension, but time. As we move into the future, its radius gets bigger

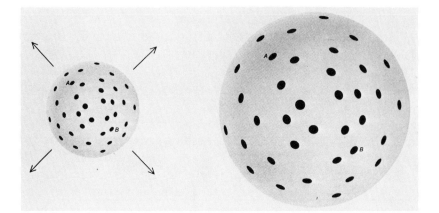

The balloon model of the universe illustrates how space expands uniformly in all directions. In this model, the three dimensions of the real world are compressed into two dimensions on the surface of a balloon. The balloon's radius represents time. Each dot on the surface of the balloon corresponds to a galaxy. As the balloon inflates (*right*), the distance between any two dots increases at a rate proportional to that distance. Each dot seems to be at the center of the expansion because it sees every other dot receding from it. *Courtesy of Scientific American.*

and the distance between specks on the surface increases. At this point, we must caution ourselves never to think of the balloon model as two-dimensional space embedded in a three-dimensional universe (for example, the room in which it is contained). The balloon *is* the universe. The balloon *is* all of space and time, not merely a universe embedded in space and time. We can not possibly step outside the real universe—outside of space and time—to take a grandstand view.

During the late 1920s, astronomers Edwin Hubble and Milton Humason demonstrated that the speed with which other galaxies appear to be receding increases proportionally with their distance from us. For example, the Hydra cluster galaxy, some 3.96 billion light years away (the American billion, used throughout this book, is equivalent to 1,000 million) is retreating at approximately 61,000 kilometers (37,912 miles) per second, or approximately 20 percent the speed of light; meanwhile, the Quasar OH471, roughly 16 billion light years away, displays one of the highest redshifts ever recorded and clocks in at the prodigious speed of just over 90 percent that of light. Yet we on Earth perceive ourselves as standing almost perfectly still. However, as Albert Einstein pointed out early in this century, our vision of the universe must not depend on who we happen to be, where we happen to be, or how we happen to be moving.

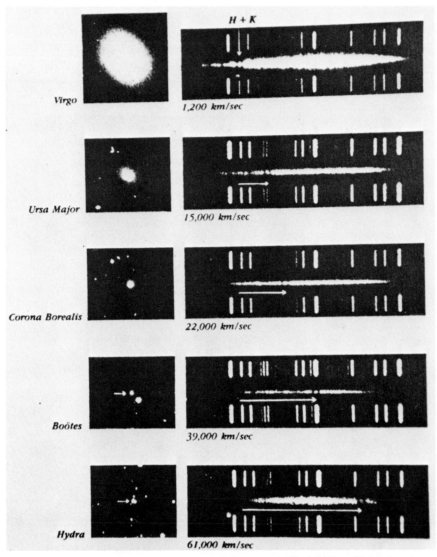

Five galaxies and their spectra, showing redshift of the *H* and *K* lines (indicated by the lengthening arrow in each successive photograph). Shifts toward the red end of the spectrum result from the stretching of wavelengths as light passes through expanding space; and the amount of redshift seen for any galaxy is proportional to its distance from the observer. *Courtesy of Hale Observatories.*

Our perception of position in the universe is not unique. If there are observers with telescopes and spectrographs on a planet in a galaxy located midway between the Milky Way and Quasar OH471, they might perceive themselves as standing still, while our galaxy and Quasar OH471 recede from them in opposite directions, each at red-

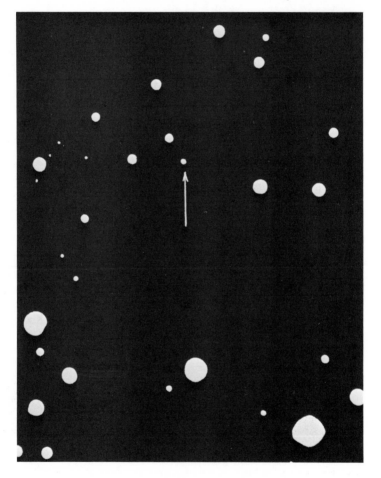

The quasar OH471 has one of the highest redshifts ever recorded. The quasar is seen receding from the Earth at a velocity slightly less than the speed of light. The Hubble constant, which equates recessional velocity with distance, is approximately 17 kilometers (10.6 miles) per second per million light years. If this constant is correct, Quasar OH471 must be 16 billion light years away; and it follows that the universe is at least 16 billion years old. *Courtesy of Hale Observatories.*

shifts approaching 45 percent the speed of light. An alien astronomer watching from Quasar OH471, looking toward the Milky Way, would see himself exactly as we see ourselves: His vantage point would seem to be located at the center of an expanding universe and, just as we see a galaxy located midway between us trailing behind him at 45 percent the speed of light, he would observe that same galaxy traveling at the same speed but in the opposite direction—toward us. And from where he stands, we ourselves appear to be traveling at 90 percent the speed of light! Yes, the Earth beneath your feet, immersed in expanding space, is retreating from Quasar OH471 at almost 269,350 kilometers (167,400 miles) per second. In fact, more distant observers may perceive us moving even faster than that, although we can not see or feel ourselves doing so.*

In essence, your perception of time and space and motion depends upon where you happen to be sitting and watching from; and paradoxes arise when ground-based observers are permitted to get into the act. Addressing this problem, Albert Einstein once said:

When a man sits with a pretty girl for an hour, it seems like a minute. But let him sit on a hot stove for a minute—and it's longer than any hour. That's relativity.

What does all this say about the origin of the universe? If the contents of the heavens are receding from each other at velocities ap-

---

* The theory of an explosive birth for the universe suggests that distant objects are moving away from us much more slowly now than they were in the past. The reason is that the tug of gravity from all directions might have slowed their motion. Because Quasar OH471 is approximately 16 billion light years away, it has taken light from the quasar that many years to reach Earth. When we look out into space, we are also looking back in time. Hence, Quasar OH471 is no longer located where we see it today, and it may indeed be traveling at a slower velocity than we record for it. But the implication that very distant objects are moving away from us at or near the speed of light is not necessarily false. If we return to our model of an inflating balloon and place a dot on that balloon to represent the Milky Way galaxy, and then a second dot about one inch (approximately 2.5 centimeters) away to represent a second galaxy, and a third dot 100 inches away from the first, the dot farthest down range from the Milky Way will always be seen receding 100 times faster than the one almost right on top of us, regardless of the rate of inflation at any given time. Points beyond the third dot, of course, would recede progressively faster, as would objects beyond Quasar OH471. In the case of the balloon—unlike the universe—we are able to observe all points in their *actual* positions, without any time delay for the passage of light from one dot to the other. The cosmic redshift results from the stretching of wavelengths as radiation moves from point to point through expanding space.

proaching and perhaps reaching the speed of light, then it follows that 60 seconds ago the most distant objects we know were some 16–18 million kilometers (approximately 10–11 million miles) closer than they are now. On the day you were born, receding clusters of galaxies must have been nearer than they are today. Working backward from your birth date, past the industrial revolution, the pharaohs of Egypt, the reign of dinosaurs, and even the appearance of our solar system, your imagination carries the galaxies closer and closer together; until finally, between 16 and 20 billion years ago, they became superimposed on top of each other in a universe that was very dense, very hot, and very simple.

This was the early universe.

We began at the bottom of a dark, backward abyss, in a state of apparently infinite density, wherein the traditional notions of space and time simply did not apply.

One day it all came apart, and the universe was never as simple again. During that first chip of time—the moment we refer to as the *Big Bang*—a compressed but rapidly expanding universe became filled with energy and particles. There occurred, if you will, a universal deluge—a splash, of sorts—with particles of matter emerging from the flood.

To come face to face with the Big Bang, you need only imagine yourself anywhere on the surface of our rubber balloon. Stay there. Then, by decreasing its radius (traveling back in time), the galaxies will approach you, shifting toward the blue in a universe that becomes progressively denser and hotter. You will discover, as the balloon deflates, that the Big Bang does not occur somewhere in space. It occupies the whole surface of the balloon—*all* of space. If we are assuming an infinite universe with no edge or center, then the universe will remain infinite in extent whether it happens to be contracting or emerging fresh and hot from the Big Bang. Which means that the Big Bang occurred everywhere. It burst forth from every direction at once as a mighty concussion of heat and light. After about one-hundredth of a second, the surroundings had cooled to a temperature of approximately 100 billion degrees Centigrade. Yes, *cooled* to approximately 100 billion degrees Centigrade, which was too hot for the first particles—photons, neutrinos, electrons, and positrons, mostly—to have

COSMIC TIME	YEARS AGO	EPOCH	EVENT
0		SINGULARITY	BIG BANG
10^{-43} SECOND		PLANCK TIME	PARTICLE CREATION
10^{-6} SECOND		HADRONIC ERA	ANNIHILATION OF PROTON-ANTIPROTON PAIRS
1 SECOND		LEPTONIC ERA	ANNIHILATION OF ELECTRON-POSITRON PAIRS
1 MINUTE		RADIATION ERA	NUCLEOSYNTHESIS OF HELIUM AND DEUTERIUM
1 WEEK			RADIATION THERMALIZES PRIOR TO THIS EPOCH
10,000 YEARS		MATTER ERA	UNIVERSE BECOMES MATTER-DOMINATED
300,000 YEARS		DECOUPLING ERA	UNIVERSE BECOMES TRANSPARENT
$1-2 \times 10^9$ YEARS			GALAXIES BEGIN TO FORM
3×10^9 YEARS			GALAXIES BEGIN TO CLUSTER
	16×10^9		OUR PROTOGALAXY COLLAPSES
	15.9×10^9		FIRST STARS FORM
	15×10^9		QUASARS ARE BORN; POPULATION II STARS FORM
	10×10^9		POPULATION I STARS FORM
	4.8×10^9		OUR PARENT INTERSTELLAR CLOUD FORMS
	4.7×10^9		COLLAPSE OF PROTOSOLAR NEBULA
	4.6×10^9		PLANETS FORM; ROCK SOLIDIFIES
	4.3×10^9		INTENSE CRATERING OF PLANETS
	3.9×10^9	ARCHEOZOIC ERA	OLDEST TERRESTRIAL ROCKS FORM
	3.5×10^9		MICROSCOPIC LIFE FORMS
	2×10^9	PROTEROZOIC ERA	OXYGEN-RICH ATMOSPHERE DEVELOPS
	1×10^9		MACROSCOPIC LIFE FORMS
	600×10^6	PALEOZOIC ERA	EARLIEST FOSSIL RECORD
	450×10^6		FIRST FISHES
	400×10^6		EARLY LAND PLANTS
	300×10^6		FERNS, CONIFERS
	200×10^6	MESOZOIC ERA	FIRST MAMMALS
	150×10^6		FIRST BIRDS
	60×10^6	CENOZOIC ERA	FIRST PRIMATES
	50×10^6		MAMMALS INCREASE
	1×10^5		HOMO SAPIENS

Major events in the history of the universe can be traced back to the Planck barrier, which marks the first one-billion-trillionth of a second, when the density of the universe was 1 followed by 94 zeros times the density of water. At the Planck barrier lies chaos; submicroscopic fluctuations rage across compressed space and time. One second later, thinned by expansion, the density of the universe was 100,000 times that of water, and its temperature was 10 billion °C. From this era of warring matter and antimatter emerged the hydrogen and helium nuclei that ultimately became us.

any stable existence at all. They were annihilated as soon as they appeared.

In the caldron of creation, the storm raged on. After about fourteen seconds the temperature had dropped to almost 3 billion degrees Centigrade, which was cool enough for electrons (negatively charged particles that orbit almost like planets around the nuclei of atoms) and positrons (the positively charged antimatter counterparts of electrons) to be created without being immediately blasted out of existence by the surrounding temperatures and pressures. They found and annihilated each other instead—a sort of matter-antimatter war—and the fact that *we are here* can only mean that the antiparticles were outnumbered. When the war ended, almost three-and-one-half minutes later, the universe had cooled to one billion degrees Centigrade, which permitted the union of protons (positively charged particles located at the centers of atoms) and neutrons (electrically neutral particles, also located at the centers of atoms).

The simplest atomic nucleus consists of a single proton. This is the nucleus of the hydrogen atom, which today constitutes approximately 90 percent of all matter in the universe. After hydrogen, the simplest (and most abundant) atomic nucleus is helium, which consists of two protons and two neutrons joined by the so-called "strong force" (which governs the union of protons and neutrons). Together, hydrogen and helium constitute approximately 99 percent of the substance of the universe. These two simplest-of-all elements were the first to be formed as radiation gave way to matter. 700,000 years after the Big Bang, the radiation background had cooled to a point that enabled nuclei to strip passing electrons from their surroundings and become the first actual atoms of hydrogen and helium gas.

This is the current story of how the world began. The experiments we have designed to test the story have failed to dislodge it—so far. This is not to say that the Big Bang theory will never be modified on the basis of new information or, at worst, thrown overboard altogether. If a new understanding does eventually force us to modify or

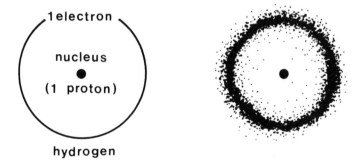

hydrogen

Hydrogen, the simplest atom, consists of a single proton and an orbiting electron. The electron is attracted to the proton by its positive charge, and assumes a sphere-shaped orbital, traveling so fast that it can be regarded as being at all points around the nucleus at once. The orbital or electron cloud shown at the right illustrates the locations *most likely* to be occupied by the electron at any given time (shown as regions of deepest shape).

abandon the Big Bang theory, we will discover that we have effectively doubled the size of the original problem. Such circumstances would be no cause for dispair. On the contrary, after we recovered from the initial shock, we would approach the problem with new questions, which would lead to new answers, which would lead to new questions. But for the time being the model endures; and in doing so it generates enough questions to keep scientists, poets, philosophers, and theologians busy for as long as the age of inquiry shall last.

2
A Fall of Hydrogen

Scientists? They believe in nothing! They believe that we are the ultimate product of a Big Bang . . . which took place in no particular place, from nothing, and for no particular reason.

The Christchurch Wizard

The shortest distance between two points is a curved line.

Albert Einstein

Seven-hundred thousand years passed, and the universe became dominated by matter: hydrogen, mostly, with some helium and possibly a trace of lithium and one or two heavier elements scattered here and there. According to all available evidence, the early universe did not remain hot enough and dense enough long enough for the heavy elements such as carbon, iron, thorium, and uranium to be assembled from primordial protons and neutrons. Hence, in the beginning there was hydrogen, and not very much of anything else.

Slowly, silently, gravity began to take over. As the gases expanded and cooled, there occurred condensations, compressions, and sub-condensations, which pulled the hydrogen and helium together into vast clouds or clumps that became the seeds of galaxies. Probably, this happened when the universe was about 2 billion years old (give or take a billion years). Here, at last, we can begin to focus attention on our own galaxy: a single 100,000 light-year-wide speck on the skin of the cosmic balloon. At first there were no stars—no lights in the heavens.

Schematic models of hydrogen and helium atoms. The hydrogen atom, consisting of a single proton and an orbiting electron, has an atomic weight of 1.0079 atomic mass units (amu). Atoms of helium contain two each of protons, neutrons, and electrons. Helium has an atomic weight of 4.0026 amu.

Nothing but the cold and the dark. Nothing but hydrogen, helium, gravity, and tomorrow.

Every atom has gravity. In that short phrase, in that single fact, lies the very basis of our existence. It means, just for a start, that matter bends or distorts the space surrounding it (*Matter bends what?*). We admit that the last sentence can be quite a mouthful to swallow without an explanation. So imagine, if you will, a region in the universe completely free of matter. In such a place, in the absence of planets and other sources of gravity, space and time are perfectly flat. A billiard ball thrown in any direction will travel forever in a strait line. Another billiard ball, left alone in one spot, will hang in place without direction or velocity for all eternity. Now, for sheer simpli-

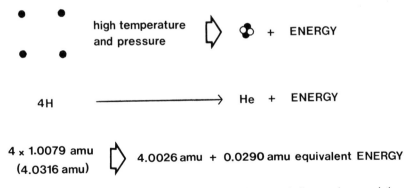

Hydrogen fusion involves the union of four protons to form one helium nucleus consisting of two protons and two neutrons. One helium nucleus is lighter than four hydrogen nuclei. The missing 0.029 amu are shed as energy.

city's sake, let us squeeze three-dimensional space down into two dimensions and imagine it as the surface of a trampoline. We quickly discover that our billiard balls are behaving in the same way as they would in a "flat" region of the universe: Shot across the canvass, one ball travels in a strait line; left sitting in one place, the other ball stays there. But if we send a very fat man out into the middle of the trampoline, the geometry of its surface changes around him: He forms a depression on the canvass, a gravitational dimple or curvature in the fabric of the trampoline. A billiard ball passing near him will find its path changed by the curved terrain that surrounds his body; and if it approaches too close or too slowly, it may get stuck in the dimple, orbiting for a while, perhaps, and eventually coming to rest at his feet. Indeed, as Albert Einstein showed us in 1915: *Matter tells spacetime how to curve, and curved spacetime tells matter how to behave.*

Thus, matter clumps together by falling into gravitational dimples of its own creation. The billiard balls in our trampoline model are themselves objects with mass and are therefore capable of creating visible dimples of their own (given a trampoline with a flexible-enough surface). Should the balls come into such close association with each other, that the edges of their dimples touch, a mutual downgrade will result and they will roll toward each other until they meet at its center. If we take these same two billiard balls out into space, away from the influence of stars and planets, and place them a few centimeters apart, the same thing will happen: They will fall down each other's gravitational dimples, slowly at first, and then come to rest side by side.

Similarly, every hydrogen atom in our protogalaxy possessed its own weak gravitational field, which added up to uncountable trillions upon trillions (the American-French trillion, which is used here, is equivalent to 1 followed by 12 zeros) of tiny dimples or chuckholes in the fabric of space and time. The protogalaxy must have been streaked with regions of greater and lesser density. Those regions with the highest populations of hydrogen and helium atoms also had the greatest number of gravitational dimples. Consequently, a hydrogen atom straying into such a neighborhood might have found itself entering a celestial obstacle course (there were a great many chuckholes in its way), a no-man's-land from which it would never emerge. Contributing its own gravitational field, the newcomer assisted in the trapping of other stray atoms, which in turn made the local gravity even stronger, which in turn attracted even more atoms.

As high-density regions (which, incidentally, were many thousands of times thinner than the air we breathe) continued to grow stronger, stripping away more and more material from their surroundings, they became unable to support their own weight. Gravitational dimples merged and became actual wells; and in many places, all at once, matter began to pour down those wells. Dense clouds broke up into shrinking globules, each caving in under its own weight and contracting toward a single, dense point. Just as the early universe became cooler as its energy and matter were spread out over the expanding dimensions of space, so the squeezing together of atoms inside contracting globules caused temperatures to rise at an ever accelerating rate. Sucking and dragging through space, the in-falling spheres of gas began to glow: red at first, then yellow, then white hot.

When matter is burned, as in a candle or by the frictional heating of an in-falling hydrogen cloud, a little bit of its mass disappears and gets converted into energy. In the case of the candle or of the hot glow of a globule-turned-protostar, the amount of matter converted to energy is only a few parts per billion. During the Second World War, our knowledge of heavy, neutron-emitting metals permitted us to make the matter-to-energy conversion much more effectively—up to a few parts per thousand. And in the summer of 1945, that lesson was driven home in a way that no human being will ever forget. A few years later we learned how to squeeze hydrogen nuclei together to make helium nuclei, which were lighter than the sum of their individual parts. This process, for better or for worse, is called fusion, and results in a matter-to-energy conversion of almost one percent.

What is the meaning of one percent of a hydrogen atom? It means that a little bit of matter is equal to an extraordinary amount of energy. For example, a hydrogen-fusion reaction small enough to be contained in a teacup, if allowed to rage as an uncontrolled nuclear storm in the heart of Manhattan, would cause the Verrazano Narrows Bridge, which is several kilometers away, to liquify instantly. The bridge would be vapor before it could fall 6 meters (20 feet).

In each collapsing globule, when increasing pressures at its center had pushed the thermometer up to 10 million degrees Centigrade, a kindling temperature was reached. This was a flash point at which so many hydrogen nuclei (now stripped of their electrons) were contained in such a small volume and were accelerated to such high velocities that when they collided they stuck together and began to form helium nuclei, releasing enormous amounts of energy as they did so. The core of the globule rebounded from the crush of gravity, ceasing to fall any further and blowing itself apart, but at the same time held together by the well of its creation. As the outer shells of the globule continued to rain down, a long thermonuclear explosion ensued, and the heavens became filled with light.

One by one, across the galaxy, they began to wink on. The first stars—the first *solar systems*—were forming. They were not solar systems like the one we are familiar with. Indeed, if you visited one of those ancient suns you would have seen immediately that prolonged survival was utterly out of the question. Quite simply, there was nothing on which to survive. If it were within your power to scour an entire solar system for all the elements heavier than helium and then to gather them together in one place, you might have been able to make a single rock. There were no solid planetary surfaces anywhere. Nor were there any rings, moons, or comets; certainly there was no oxygen to breathe, for it did not even exist yet; and no water, no ice, no food of any kind.

You might be wondering what there *was*. Many stars existed. In fact, many new ones continued to form each day from the flotsam and jetsam of the Big Bang. Companion stars circled around some, each basking in the other's rays. Planets orbited around other suns. These planets would have been the Jupiters of their solar systems, lacking sufficient mass to become full-fledged stars. Unlike Jupiter, their cloudtops were not streaked with nitrogen and water vapor and hydrocarbons; you could dive clear through the core of one of those worlds without ever encountering anything other than hydrogen and helium. Their atmospheres alive with lightning, they circled their suns at immense distances, coasting on the frontiers of the night. No giant, gassy worlds ranging near a central sun, in orbits comparable to those of Mars, Earth, Venus, or Mercury, survived the ignition of its nuclear fires: At the moment a star came to life, its heat and light began to erode the inner planets, whose gases blazed and streamed away into space like the tails of mighty comets. Their substance was lost in the greater reaches of the solar system. Since they contained no rocky cores, they boiled away completely, leaving a huge, empty gap between each star and its outer, frozen gas giants.

If you could venture back to that time, you would find hydrogen and helium thrown everywhere. Our own solar system would not even be born for several billions of years. But you could easily notice bright amber, scarlet, and turquoise points of light; and from them you might guess that life in the universe was really about to start.

3
The Emergence of Carbon

I remember seeing the stars and asking my friends what they were. They told me that they were lights in the sky.

Carl Sagan

Impure. Contaminated. These words define the end of all stars: the appearance and proliferation of foreign elements in their interiors. Dark and heavy, the atomic nuclei of carbon, oxygen, and iron are the cancers of suns. The delicate balancing act between gravity and the fusion reactions seeking to blow a star apart can not possibly last forever. Sooner or later, gravity is bound to win. Its unfailing grip force-feeds the thermonuclear fires, yet at the same time it holds the resulting explosion together. We have seen that hydrogen-fusion burning produces helium nuclei as an end product or residuum. Eventually, most of the hydrogen in the core is fused into helium, and hydrogen-fusion burning begins to slow down. As the explosions weaken, gravity tightens its fist and collapses the star further. It compresses the star's helium-rich center and causes temperatures to soar until helium-fusion burning is ignited, producing a new outpouring of energy that temporarily halts any further collapse.

The residua of helium-fusion burning are carbon and oxygen nuclei, and the emergence of these elements signals the star's impending death. When the helium is exhausted, the star will contract once again. At this point, either the star convulses violently, peeling off and throwing its outermost envelopes of hydrogen and helium into space;

or, if it has a mass of twenty or more times that of our sun, the contraction many continue, with temperatures rising steadily until the transformation of carbon into heavier elements begins. Still later, when temperatures at the core have risen to one billion degrees Centigrade, oxygen-fusion burning is ignited.

A feature common to all these reactions is that they liberate energy. In each case, heavy elements are fused to form still heavier elements, so that the star begins to develop a series of fusion-burning shells, with the heaviest and hottest of them residing deep within. The bright flame of carbon-fusion burning eventually becomes sandwiched between down-pressing helium and a deepening sea of oxygen. We are now looking at a highly evolved star, with four major fusion-burning reactions occurring simultaneously at its core: a four-fold seething hotbed whose radiations gently nudge the uppermost shells of hydrogen outward toward cold space. The star has swollen to red giantism.

The end products of carbon- and oxygen-fusion burning are not as simple as those of the hydrogen and helium pathways. As described in chapters 1 and 2, atomic nuclei are built from protons and neutrons, and the mass of an atomic nucleus is less than the mass of the protons and neutrons from which it is constructed. The difference is expressed as an outpouring of energy, which is released when the nucleus is formed. In the beginning of the star's life, when there were only hydrogen nuclei to work with, the end products of fusion burning were helium nuclei. Once helium-fusion burning was ignited, three helium nuclei could be combined to form a single carbon nucleus, and the addition of a fourth often gave rise to oxygen: The star's core became a ball of carbon and oxygen. Heated to one-half-billion degrees Centigrade, carbon nuclei pair up and fuse with each other, sometimes shedding hydrogen and helium as by-products to produce such elements as neon, sodium, and magnesium. The fractional loss of mass, and the resultant yield of energy from the formation of each nucleus, is higher for carbon-carbon fusion than for helium-helium-helium fusion; the accompanying heat gain forces an uneasy marriage between pairs of oxygen nuclei, which beget silicon, phosphorus, and sulfur. Hence, the residua of carbon- and oxygen-fusion burning are silicon and its neighbors in the periodic table of the elements.

At 1 billion degrees Centigrade, an oxygen-fusion burning core creeps outward, away from the center; it is nurtured by a steady rain

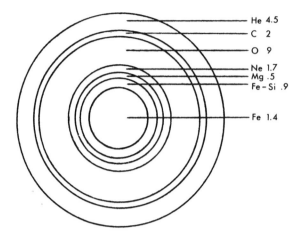

He 4.5
C 2
O 9
Ne 1.7
Mg .5
Fe – Si .9
Fe 1.4

The structure of a very old star with a mass twenty times that of the sun, showing multiple shell burning. Elements heavier than helium are synthesized by fusion-burning reactions deep within massive stars. Iron will not fuse, and its accumulation at the core renders the star unstable, eventually triggering a supernova explosion, which in turn leads to the synthesis of still heavier elements. The star depicted here has transmuted virtually all of its hydrogen into heavy elements. Elemental abundances are shown in units of the sun's mass.

of oxygen nuclei and deposits behind itself an ever-growing lump of silicon and other impurities, including fluorine, which is the residuum of oxygen-phosphorus fusion.

A quiver. The oxygen-fusion burning reactions are failing. Gravity closes its fist once more, squeezing the interior, forcing temperatures up to 3 billion degrees Centigrade, and triggering a complex series of reactions called silicon-burning.

The "silicon peak elements," so called because of the relative abundance of silicon and its neighbors throughout this part of the universe, do not fuse easily, at least not at a mere 3 billion degrees Centigrade. Their nuclei are too massive and tend to repel each other. Instead, an alpha particle (a positively charged particle consisting of two protons and two neutrons, which is, in essence, the nucleus of a helium atom) may be chipped off a silicon or phosphorus nucleus and added to a sulfur nucleus, or vice versa, so that nuclei are continually breaking apart and exchanging their pieces to create such large, heavy elements as chromium, manganese, iron, cobalt, and nickel (the "iron peak elements").

Now, a very dense, hot lump dominated by iron nuclei begins to ac-

IA	IIA	IIIB	IVB	VB	VIB	VIIB	VIII			IB	IIB	IIIA	IVA	VA	VIA	VIIA	NOBLE GASES
1 H 1.00797 ±0.00001																	2 He 4.0026 ±0.0005
3 Li 6.939 ±0.0005	4 Be 9.0122 ±0.00005											5 B 10.811 ±0.003	6 C 12.0115 ±0.0005	7 N 14.0067 ±0.00005	8 O 15.9994 ±0.0001	9 F 18.9984 ±0.001	10 Ne 20.183 ±0.0005
11 Na 22.9898 ±0.00005	12 Mg 24.312 ±0.0005											13 Al 26.9815 ±0.00005	14 Si 28.086 ±0.005	15 P 30.9738 ±0.00005	16 S 32.064 ±0.003	17 Cl 35.453 ±0.001	18 Ar 39.948 ±0.005
19 K 39.102 ±0.005	20 Ca 40.08 ±0.005	21 Sc 44.956 ±0.0005	22 Ti 47.90 ±0.005	23 V 50.942 ±0.0005	24 Cr 51.996 ±0.001	25 Mn 54.9380 ±0.00005	26 Fe 55.847 ±0.003	27 Co 58.9332 ±0.0005	28 Ni 58.71 ±0.005	29 Cu 63.54 ±0.005	30 Zn 65.37 ±0.005	31 Ga 69.72 ±0.005	32 Ge 72.59 ±0.005	33 As 74.9216 ±0.00005	34 Se 78.96 ±0.005	35 Br 79.909 ±0.002	36 Kr 83.80 ±0.005
37 Rb 85.47 ±0.005	38 Sr 87.62 ±0.005	39 Y 88.905 ±0.0005	40 Zr 91.22 ±0.005	41 Nb 92.906 ±0.0005	42 Mo 95.94 ±0.005	43 Tc (99)	44 Ru 101.07 ±0.005	45 Rh 102.905 ±0.0005	46 Pd 106.4 ±0.05	47 Ag 107.870 ±0.003	48 Cd 112.40 ±0.005	49 In 114.82 ±0.005	50 Sn 118.69 ±0.005	51 Sb 121.75 ±0.005	52 Te 127.60 ±0.005	53 I 126.9044 ±0.0005	54 Xe 131.30 ±0.005
55 Cs 132.905 ±0.0005	56 Ba 137.34 ±0.005	57 La 138.91 ±0.005	72 Hf 178.49 ±0.005	73 Ta 180.948 ±0.0005	74 W 183.85 ±0.005	75 Re 186.2 ±0.05	76 Os 190.2 ±0.05	77 Ir 192.2 ±0.05	78 Pt 195.09 ±0.005	79 Au 196.967 ±0.0005	80 Hg 200.59 ±0.005	81 Tl 204.37 ±0.005	82 Pb 207.19 ±0.005	83 Bi 208.980 ±0.0005	84 Po (210)	85 At (210)	86 Rn (222)
87 Fr (223)	88 Ra (226)	89 Ac (227)	104 Rf	105 Ha	106												

Lanthanum Series

58 Ce 140.12 ±0.005	59 Pr 140.907 ±0.0005	60 Nd 144.24 ±0.005	61 Pm (147)	62 Sm 150.35 ±0.005	63 Eu 151.96 ±0.005	64 Gd 157.25 ±0.005	65 Tb 158.924 ±0.0005	66 Dy 162.50 ±0.005	67 Ho 164.930 ±0.0005	68 Er 167.26 ±0.005	69 Tm 168.934 ±0.0005	70 Yb 173.04 ±0.005	71 Lu 174.97 ±0.005

Actinium Series

90 Th 232.038 ±0.0005	91 Pa (231)	92 U 238.03 ±0.005	93 Np (237)	94 Pu (242)	95 Am (243)	96 Cm (247)	97 Bk (247)	98 Cf (249)	99 Es (254)	100 Fm (253)	101 Md (256)	102 No (253)	103 Lw (257)

The periodic table of the elements. All elements can be placed in this table according to the number of protons within their nuclei (atomic number) and the arrangement of electrons in their outer shells.

cumulate at the very center of the star. It churns there, growing. But iron does not fuse, no matter how much it is squeezed or how much it is heated. If the star is 20 times the mass of our sun, the iron-rich core may swell to 1.5 solar masses. The heart of the star then becomes inert—a parasite—gorging itself on the residua of fusion burning, yet contributing nothing. The next time the thermonuclear explosions begin to falter, gravity must win. Under a tightening fist, the core of iron may become what is called degenerate gas, a state in which electrons are crowded so closely together, almost literally bumper-to-bumper, that the subatomic traffic begins to resemble a more frantic version of midtown Manhattan at rush hour. The electrons vigorously resist any further crowding, bouncing off each other, if they have to, to get wherever it is they are going. Try as they may, no two electrons (or cars) can occupy the same space. The effect is called the *Pauli exclusion principle,* and it operates when the star's central regions become so dense that a couple of teaspoonfuls of compacted stellar material weigh as much as an aircraft carrier.

At this stage, further compression of the interior (increased density)

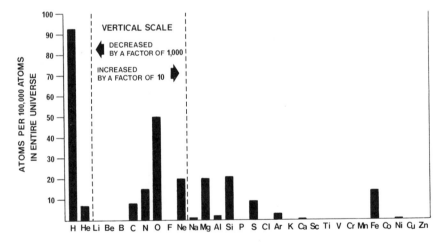

Interstellar abundances of the first thirty elements in the periodic table. The C, O, Ne, Mg, Si, S, Ar, Ca, and Fe peaks illustrate the relative abundance of elements with even atomic numbers (elements whose nuclei contain an even number of protons). This is because the thermonuclear reactions that synthesize heavy elements within stars tend to use the helium nucleus as a building block. Beryllium is scarce because helium-fusion burning favors the fusion of three helium nuclei to form carbon over the reaction that stops with the formation of beryllium from two helium nuclei. *Based on data from Hoyle and Wickramasinghe, 1979.*

continues to push the pressure to new heights, but the temperature begins to change almost independently of the pressure. It then becomes possible for the density and pressure to fly upward under the crush of gravity while the temperature lags far behind or even falls. When this happens, the star is finished. Electrons actually get squashed inside iron nuclei, some of them shattering against positively charged protons and combining with them to form neutrons. With barely a shudder of resistance, the core begins to shrink, receding from the outer shells. More and more matter rushes down toward the center, piling higher and higher and gaining momentum, until the core becomes a monstrous wave front converging from every direction at once on a single, central point. Exactly what happens when the wave reaches the center is not well understood. During a few brief moments, the amount of energy radiated from the core exceeds the energy output of an entire galaxy of stars. An atomic nucleus residing in one of the star's outer shells might as well be a flea located in the mouth of a shotgun. The shells explode away from a raw, violet-white center, ripping completely apart and gushing up into outer space at a small fraction of the speed of light—a *supernova.*

Just as the detonation of a very large star may blow many times our sun's mass off into space, deep down, at the center of the star, matter may be imploded down to a 32 kilometer (20 mile) wide ball of shoulder-to-shoulder neutrons (thus creating a neutron star). Or, if the explosion is powerful enough, particles may be squeezed below the operating limit of the *Pauli exclusion principle* (known as the Chandrasekhar limit), so that the neutrons themselves come to pieces, shattering and diving into themselves until all the materials of the star's core are contained in a dense lump that would be dwarfed by a virus; this lump is smaller, in fact, than the realm of distances measurable by the most powerful microscopes that will ever be built. The center of the star has then become a *singularity,* a cosmic "free-fire" zone, wrapped in slowed time and curved space.

Above the star's imploding heart, the out-flying shells of iron and silicon peak elements and helium and hydrogen are flash-fried at several billion degrees Centigrade. Then, from the depths of the *supernova* comes a tidal wave of particles, including neutrons, protons, and alpha particles (helium nuclei); these make possible a whole spectrum of rapid nuclear reactions that, except for a few specially

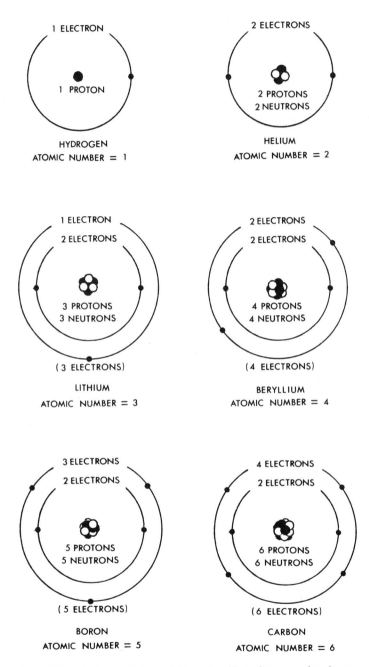

Schematic models of hydrogen, helium, lithium, beryllium, boron, and carbon atoms. The atomic number is equal to the number of protons in the nucleus of an atom.

designed particle accelerators, probably occur nowhere else in the universe. A magnesium nucleus, for example, may be struck by a neutron that sticks, then by a proton; and suddenly it is no longer magnesium but aluminum. An iron nucleus, riveted by a rapid-fire barrage of neutrons, may be turned into iridium, platinum, or gold, and gold into lead or uranium. Most of the elements between carbon and iron that are not in the silicon-iron peaks, and all of the elements heavier than nickel, are created during supernova explosions, primarily through the capture of neutrons. Later, when the ejecta of the supernova have cooled and spread into the gaps between the stars, spallation nuclear reactions (the breakdown of large nuclei by cosmic rays) lead to the formation of such rare, light elements as lithium, beryllium, and boron. These and the other elements that are not produced by fusion burning reactions prior to the supernova event are relatively scarce in our own bodies, in the Earth beneath our feet, and throughout the entire range of the visible universe.

In the cooling, off-thrown shells of an exploded star, atomic nuclei—mostly hydrogen and helium—capture passing electrons and confine them to tight spherical and dumbbell-shaped orbitals. Shimmering faintly, like glowing embers in a campfire, the wreckage of the star contains virtually every element in the periodic table, including carbon, nitrogen, oxygen, phosphorus, and sulfur.

Atoms of carbon support both an inner and an outer layer of wildly racing electrons, with the outer layer (called an electron cloud or orbital) tending to form electron transfer bonds with the outermost layers of other atoms. Plunged into a sea of hydrogen gas, a carbon

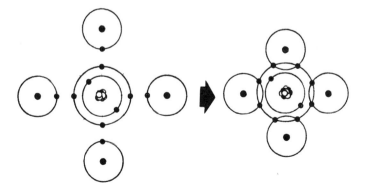

Electron sharing between four hydrogen atoms and a carbon atom to form methane (CH_4).

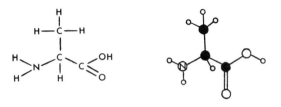

Alanine, an amino acid built from atoms of hydrogen (H), carbon (C), nitrogen (N), and oxygen (O), is presented as a structural formula (*left*) and model (*right*). Each line represents a pair of shared electrons. In the double bond (covalent bond) between oxygen and carbon, two pairs of electrons are shared.

atom provides "parking space" for four other atoms and emerges as a molecule of methane (CH_4). Carbon also joins with carbon, and can do so with single (as ethane: $H_3C - CH_3$), double (as ethene: $H_2C = CH_2$), or triple bonds (as ethyne: $HC \equiv CH$). It knits itself into long chains, freely branching constructions, wheels, coils, or clumps that incorporate nitrogen, oxygen, phosphorus, and sulfur to produce molecules containing several hundred individual parts, even in the absence of living organisms or a planet capable of supporting them. This is the substance of organic chemistry. Every portion of an amoeba, a virus, an apple, a whale, or your own body can be reduced essentially to carbon, hydrogen, nitrogen, and oxygen. As J.B.S. Haldane once observed, "Even the Archbishop of Canterbury is sixty-five percent water."

It might be concluded, then, that the phenomenon we call life originated through some of the most likely chemical changes undergone by some of the most common elements in this part of the universe. In other words, you and I and the flowers in your garden were pulled from a disarmingly small bag of tricks.

In the warm ejecta of a supernova, a little energy and a lot of matter can combine to produce reactions in which atoms link up and become molecules; and the molecules break apart and mix and rejoin in all sorts of new ways. Recent observations in radio astronomy* have confirmed an abundance of simple organic molecules in interstellar gas

---

*In radio astronomy, microwaves rather than lightwaves are collected and studied. The very short radiowaves provide an electronic spectrum whose absorption lines can be used like a fingerprint file to identify elements and molecules dispersed between the microwave source and the Earth.

Some molecules found in outer space.

COMPOUND	FORMULA	COMPOUND	FORMULA
Hydrogen	H_2	Cyanoacetylene	$HC \equiv C-C-C-N$
Hydroxyl radical	OH	Cyanogen radical	CN
water	H_2O	Hydrogen cyanide	HCN
Hydrogen sulfide	H_2S	Hydrogen isocyanide	HNC
Ammonia	NH_3	Carbonyl sulfide	$O = C = S$
Formaldehyde	H_2CO	Formamide	$HCONH_2$
Thioformaldehyde	H_2CS	Methylenimine	$H_2C = NH$
Acetaldehyde	CH_3CHO	Methylamine	CH_3NH_2
Acetonitrile	CH_3CN	Dimethyl ether	$H_3C-O-CH_3$
Acrylonitrile	$H_2C-CHCN$	Methyl formate	$HCOOCH_3$
Methanol	CH_3OH	Cyanamide	NH_2CN
Ethanol	C_2H_5OH	Ethyl cyanide	CH_3CH_2CN
Carbon monosulfide	CS	Cyanotetra acetylene	HC_9N
Carbon monoxide	CO		
Formic acid	HCOOH		
Isocyanic acid	$HN = C = O$		
Acetylene	$HC \equiv CH$		
Methyl acetylene	$HC \equiv C-CH_3$		

clouds whose contents are largely the ejecta of dead suns. The compounds observed include key steps in chemical evolution, such as hydrogen cyanide (HCN), formaldehyde (H_2CO), cyanoacetylene ($HC \equiv C-N$), formic acid (HCOOH), methylenimine ($H_2C = NH$), acetaldehyde (CH_3CHO), and acetonitrile (CH_3CN). In experiments dealing with preliving organic chemistry, purine adenine has been synthesized entirely from molecules of hydrogen cyanide; merely shining ultraviolet light on formaldehyde can incite the formation of sugars and polysaccharides (which include starch and cellulose); cyanoacetylene is an important condensing agent in preliving chemical evolution; and formic acid and methylenimine have been used to construct the simplest known amino acid, glycine, while aldehydes and nitriles appear to be the precursors of other amino acids.

One does not need to be a molecular biologist to see immediately that the progression is toward more complex organic compounds. The simplest molecules—the ones we see spread across interstellar space—might conceivably have been synthesized by condensation effects within the cooling, outracing shells of expired stars, much like the formation of water droplets within a cloud of the terrestrial atmosphere. But the brief period of bonding activity could not possibly

Atom	Symbol	Atomic Number	Electrons in Outer Shell	Biological Occurrence
Carbon	C	6	4	Basic atom of all organic compounds
Oxygen	O	8	6	Component of most biological molecules; final electron acceptor in energy-yielding reactions
Hydrogen	H	1	1	Component of most biological molecules; H^+ ion important component of solutions
Nitrogen	N	7	5	Component of proteins, nucleic acids, and many other biological molecules
Sulfur	S	16	6	Component of many proteins
Phosphorus	P	15	5	Component of nucleic acids and molecules carrying chemical energy; found in many lipid molecules
Iron	Fe	26	2	Important in energy-yielding reactions; component of oxygen carriers in blood
Calcium	Ca	20	2	Found in bones and teeth; important in muscle contraction
Potassium	K	19	1	Important in conduction of nerve impulses
Sodium	Na	11	1	Ion in solution in living matter
Chlorine	Cl	17	7	Ion in solution in living matter
Magnesium	Mg	12	2	Part of molecules important in photosynthesis; important ion in many enzyme-catalyzed reactions
Copper	Cu	29	1	Important in photosynthesis and energy-yielding reactions
Iodine	I	53	7	Component of hormone produced by thyroid gland
Fluorine	F	9	7	Found in trace amounts
Manganese	Mn	25	2	Found in trace amounts
Zinc	Zn	30	2	Found in trace amounts
Selenium	Se	34	6	Found in trace amounts
Molybdenum	Mo	42	1	Found in trace amounts

Some important atoms in living oranisms. *From* Biology: the Foundations *by Stephen L. Wolfe.* © *1077 by Wadsworth Publishing Company, Inc. Reprinted by permission of Wadsworth Publishing Company, Belmont, California 94002.*

have lasted very long. Expansion and rarefaction of the ejected matter, accompanied by steadily dropping temperatures, would have dictated that organic synthesis grind to a halt.

What next? you might ask. Unfortunately, it is difficult to say with any certainty because so little is currently known about interstellar clouds. Many of the atoms probably condense out as frozen grains of graphite and water (''dirty ice''), trapping organic molecules inside their mantles and on their surfaces. Cornell University astronomer Carl Sagan has suggested the operation of what he calls "a kind of ultraviolet natural selection in the interstellar medium," by which those molecules that are stable against the destructive effects of interstellar ultraviolet radiation may eventually achieve significant abundance, even if their rate of production is very slow. He predicts a trend toward high-molecular-weight material, stating simply that large molecules are, all other things being equal, more stable than small molecules. Clumps, bushes, and wheels appear to be the most likely shapes to endure. If a single bond is broken in a long, string-like molecule, the entire strand is cut in two and its pieces, flying off in opposite directions, are very unlikely to come back together and reassemble themselves as the original molecule; but if the same bond is broken in a bush- or ring-shaped molecule, the adjacent atoms will hold the severed ends in place and the break will heal. In addition, flattened, ring-shaped organic molecules, because of the bridge-like structure of their electron clouds, are able to absorb in the ultraviolet, as an excitation rather than a dissociation event, and may in fact function as primitive energy-storing molecules. For these reasons, Dr. Sagan observes, cyclic compounds of high molecular weight may be a major constituent of interstellar grains and gas.

And here, at this early stage, before we can speak of anything even resembling life, we are talking about natural selection. Indeed, it does seem that selective forces began operating on organic molecules long before the appearance of a genetic coding system capable of reproducing itself (DNA); they began in fact, even before the appearance of Earth-like planets in our galaxy.

Heavy atoms, coughed out into space by stars, provide the raw materials. A single carbon atom can join with a single oxygen atom in only one way: to produce carbon monoxide (CO). Introduce four hydrogen atoms and the number of possible combinations broadens to include methane (CH_4), water (H_2O), formaldehyde (H_2CO), and methanol (CH_3OH), each with very unique properties, as a simple taste-test would demonstrate. Every time a new atom is introduced, the number of potential end products is miltiplied; thus, spreading before us in the gas and the dust, lie infinite possibilities. The environment between the stars can be likened to the role of an executioner, drawing and quartering and dissociating those molecules that are "unfit," while Carl Sagan's rings express their superiority over the long, stringy, single bonded compounds as differential rates of survival.*

Fred Hoyle and Chandra Wickramasinghe of University College, Cardiff, Wales, believe—perhaps a little optimistically—that cold and extraordinarily diffuse interstellar clouds need not be dead-end zones for preliving chemical evolution. They suggest instead that an abundance of solid grains, organic compounds, atoms and molecules with unpaired electrons (free radicals), electrically charged atoms (ions), ultraviolet photons, and a wide range of temperatures (varying according to the nearness of stars) provide ideal conditions for the assembly of exotic molecular species, with natural selection acting on the assembled products. Hoyle sees the emergence and survival of complex molecules able to reproduce themselves, from which even life could develop. There exists only one major hurdle to this theory, but this one is quite enough: that very large quantities of hydrogen, carbon, nitrogen, oxygen, phosphorus, and sulfur must be brought together and kept together, then heated at just the right temperature for a long time before anything resembling even a chlorophyll molecule, much less a self reproducing virus particle, will be evolved. Gases ejected from supernovas do not remain dense and warm long enough to permit the formation of very elaborate compounds; and by the time they spread into the interstellar medium, the shells are at least several million times thinner than the air you are presently breathing. When gas clouds do become dense enough to sustain the building of more complex organic molecules, they tend also to grow unstable against gravity. Unable to support their own weight, they collapse, breaking up into globules which spill into themselves and become stars and planets. That's exactly what happened right here, near the rim of the galaxy, about 5 billion years ago.

And that's when all the excitement started.

---

* Norman Macbeth and others have argued that differential survival, the so-called "survival of the fittest," amounts to a tautology, a needless repitition of the same idea, which only says that "those who survive, survive because they are the fittest, and the fittest are the fittest because they survive." In other words, natural selection, as critics of Darwinian evolution delight in pointing out, means little more than "the survival of those who survive." Thus, when we speak of differential survival, we might as well be saying that black paper is dark-colored; the phrase means no more than "black paper is dark because it is black." But there is an important difference here. Black paper is dark simply by definition of its being black, whereas the survival of a population, whether it be a population of molecules or of serpents, is a *result*, not a *definition*, of its potential for survival.

4
From Stardust

When I meet the maker of the universe, I would like to be able to tell Him a little of how it works.

John D. Isaacs

Here we are, living on the solar system's fattest collection of rocks, whirling around a very average star. That star is part of a galaxy that includes a couple of hundred stars for each man, woman, and child on Earth; and beyond our own little island of suns lie a hundred billion other galaxies, each with anywhere from a few million to a few trillion stars, and each about the same age as our galaxy. Altogether there are an estimated 10,000,000,000,000,000,000,000 stars in the universe, and if, as is currently believed, planets are a normal by-product of star formation, then there are almost ten times that many worlds (add another zero).

As we have seen in the previous chapter, the heavier elements in the galaxy—the stuff from which worlds, diamonds, viruses, *Homo sapiens,* and skyscrapers are made—accumulated from the debris of supernova explosions. The life span of a star is dependent upon its mass. The more massive a star, the greater the influence of gravity, which adds up to a greater amount of heat and pressure deep within, which in turn quickens the tempo of fusion burning.

If our sun—a rather medium-sized star—is destined to consume most of its hydrogen content during a lifetime of 10 billion years or so, a star with a mass 30 times greater will use up its nuclear fuel in only

The Crab nebula as seen through the 200-inch telescope on Polomar Mountain. Chinese records indicate that the supernova giving rise to the nebula erupted in our skies on the morning of July 4, A.D. 1054. Located at a distance of 6,000 light years in the constellation Taurus, the Crab measures nearly six light years across. The gases are spreading outward from the explosion-center at approximately 1390 kilometers (864 miles) per second. They have become available matter for the formation of future stars and planets. Hale Observatories, California Institute of Technology.

one million years (we call upon you, the reader, to bear with us; astronomers, geologists, and biologists have a peculiar way of viewing time), dying violently and scattering most of its mass into space.

In approximately 4945 B.C., almost 1,800 years before the first dynasties of Egypt, a massive star in the constellation of Taurus erupted into a supernova. The star was almost 6,000 light years away, so the flash from the explosion was not seen on Earth until July 4 in A.D. 1054, as recorded by the Chinese historian Toktaga in *History of the Sung Dynasty* (part 9, chapter 56):

On a chi-chhou day in the fifth month of the first year of Chih-Ho Reign-Period a "guest star" appeared at the south-east of Thein-

Kuan, measuring several inches. After more than a year, it faded away.

The "guest star" grew bright enough to cast shadows, and for about two weeks it seemed as though the sun had gained a sister. More than 900 years later, we have come to know its gaseous remnant as the Crab nebula. Through telescopes it can be seen as a hot, expanding cloud nearly six light years across. Its ejecta are hurtling away from the center at 1,390 kilometers (864 miles) per second and, 50,000 years from now, it will have spread across 150 light years of space (approximately 0.15 percent the diameter of the galaxy).

One million years after the first stars appeared in our galaxy, supernovas began pumping heavy elements into the interstellar medium. Present estimates suggest that there is probably one supernova in our galaxy every thirty years or so. At this rate, heavy elements in quantities suitable for the formation of rocky, Earth-like planets would have only begun to accumulate in the galaxies during the last 5 or 6 billion years. In the constellation Canis Major, which is only a few degrees from Sirius, lies an association of young, bright stars; these are new solar systems that condensed from gas and dust while *Homo erectus* was going about the business of building huts, mastering fire,

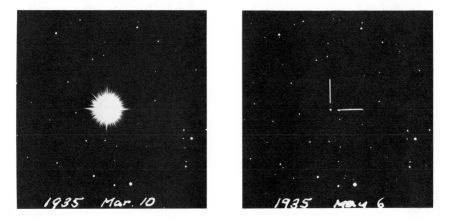

A supernova in the constellation Hercules. The view on the left shows the supernova as it appeared when first discovered in 1935. Two months later, the supernova had faded almost out of existence (*right*). Such eruptions are believed to occur in our galaxy approximately every thirty years, but many are obscured behind galactic dust clouds. *Lick Observatory Photograph.*

organizing hunts, and inventing languages and agriculture. The Earth is much older than *Homo erectus*—4.6 billion years older, if the latest clues provided by rocks from Greenland, the moon, and the Allende meteorite are to be believed. This means that Earth is not a newcomer by any stretch of the imagination. If there are other life-supporting, Earthlike planets among the stars (which, in terms of mathematics, is a certainty), then the oldest of them can not have formed much earlier than the Earth itself. To put it another way, we are among the most ancient creatures in the universe.

Stan Lee and Jack Kirby, the comic-book impresarios who made antimatter a household word, once permitted the Fabulous Fantastic Four to witness the destruction of a very old world whose fragments seeded life elsewhere in the universe. "Such is the law of the universe," a wide-eyed Johnny Storm learned. "For every beginning there is an end, and from every end there shall arise a new beginning."

Amidst all this is both analogy and irony when we consider the apparent origin of our Earth and sun. The iron pulsing through your

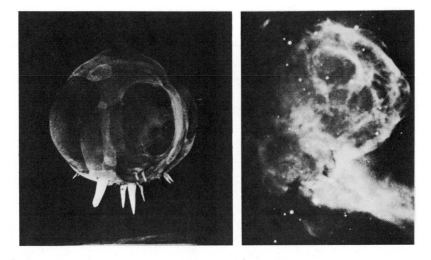

Two expanding shock bubbles. One lasted for only a few milliseconds, the other grows almost undetectably and has endured for millennia. At left is Harold E. "Doc" Edgerton's photo of an atomic explosion on a tower at Eniwetok in the Pacific. The downward spikes result from electricity running down and around guy wires. *Reprinted from* Moments of Vision *by Harold E. Edgerton by permission of The MIT Press, Cambridge, Massachusetts.* © *1979.* At right is the off-thrown shell of NGC 2359. *Courtesy of Harvard-Smithsonian Center for Astrophysics.*

veins once gushed from the heart of a dying star. Thrown into space, an expanding globe of ejected matter—the whole periodic table— burst forth at a speed of almost 10,000 kilometers (6,215 miles) per second, colliding with the rarefied gases and dust of the interstellar medium, and sweeping some of it along; it grew into a towering but decelerating monster several light years across. Nearly 5 billion years ago, one of those monsters broke against the dark cloud from which our sun developed. It contributed ejecta that had not yet thoroughly blended with the wreckage from earlier supernovas (little nuggets of this material have been found intact in certain light, crumbly meteo- rites), and it struck us like a mighty flyswatter. Where it contacted the cloud, trying to burst through to the other side, the wall of oncoming gas and dust lost much of its force, stumbling, falling against the primordial nebula, pushing it, compressing it, and possibly triggering its collapse.*

When nebula contracted, it began to fragment. The result was not one star; it was the formation of an association or cluster of about 30 stars. Yes, we have relatives—blood brothers, so to speak. And, like us, they are old. Very, very old.

More than a dozen galactic days have passed since the sun and the planets formed, a period during which the solar system made at least twelve complete revolutions around the galactic center, and also a period during which members of the original star cluster mght have wandered off in different directions. Still, one of our closest neighbors, Alpha Centauri A, outermost of the two bright pointers that guided the old mariners to the Southern Cross, might well be our sun's identical twin sister.

Evidence supporting this possibility emerged during 1980, while Australian National University astronomer Mike Bessell was studying patterns of light from nearby stars. Using specially sensitized photo- graphic plates and a telescope at the Mount Stromlo Observatory near Canberra, he obtained detailed spectral signatures from several stars

---

* We are now learning that supernova-induced star formation appears to be wide-spread in our galaxy. Current models suggest that a supernova can trigger star formation that gives rise even- tually to another supernova, which triggers more star formation, and so on, until a whole chain of star-forming regions might result; but, of course, other mechanisms (mere gravitational at- traction, for example) also contribute to the collapse of gas clouds. After all, the emergence of the very first stars is not easily explained by the supernova model.

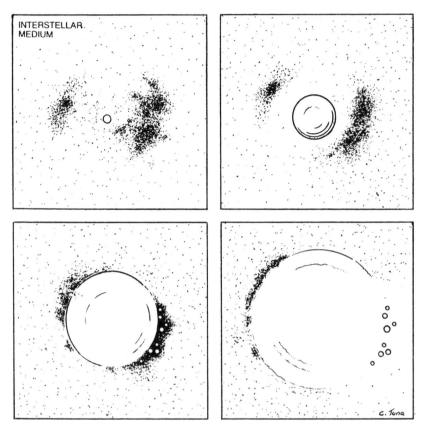

Shock fronts, racing in every direction from a supernova explosion, may induce the formation of new stars by sweeping up and compressing interstellar gas and dust to a density high enough for gravity to pull the material together. Stars forming within the in-falling clouds will occur as associations or clusters embedded in a spherical shell of slowly expanding hydrogen.

and began to compare them, hoping to reveal clues that might tell us something about the nebulae from which they condensed. Alpha Centauri A's signature, when compared with our sun's, is astonishingly similar. Says Bessell:

> The match between the two stars, demonstrated by spectrum analysis, is there in detail—even down to the unlikey ratio of one atom of iron to every 31,620 atoms of hydrogen. And the ratios are just as precise with other metals and chemicals, with the elements of titanium, calcium, nickel, zinc—even barium and lead.

Alpha Centauri A is our second nearest stellar neighbor, riding the night at a distance of 4.34 light years (approximately 25 trillion miles). If the star is our sun's twin sister (and that is a point that will be argued for many years), then it was formed on almost the same day, from the same ingredients in the same fragmenting, in-falling cloud of frozen matter. "The twin" has the same surface temperature, is almost the same size (exceeding our sun by approximately one-tenth of a solar mass), and will die only shortly before our parent star. The obvious next question is, if our sun has a twin sister 4.34 light years away,

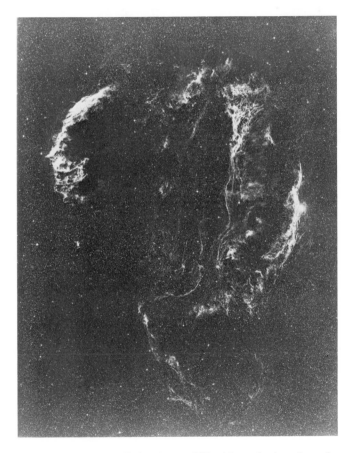

A supernova remnant in the constellation Cygnus. This whispy, glowing sphere of gas and dust, measuring 120 light years across, is the wreckage of a star that blew itself apart some 20,000 years ago. As the outracing shock bubble sweeps up and compresses cool interstellar material, it may trigger the formation of new stars. *Courtesy of Hale Observatories.*

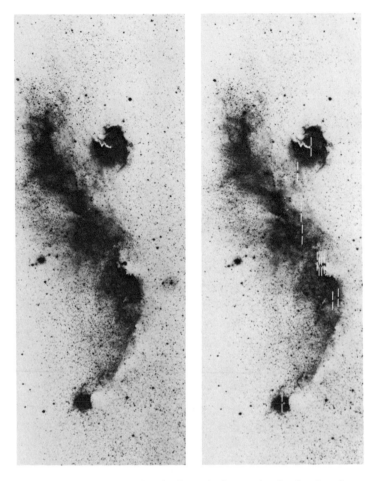

Star formation can be observed in this pair of negative images showing the edge of an expanding sphere of supernova ejecta in the constellation Canis Major. Brackets (*right*) mark associations of bright infant stars whose formation might have been triggered by the shock front; this compressed interstellar gas and dust to a sufficiently high density for gravity to pull the material together into solar systems. Evidently, this happened even as humankind was developing language and the control of fire. The arc measures nearly 100 light years from top to bottom. This photograph was made with the 48-inch Schmidt telescope on Polomar Mountain. *Courtesy of Polomar Observatory, California Institute of Technology.*

might there also be a twin Venus, Mars, or Earth? Possibly. But, like approximately half of the stars in our galaxy, which are part of binary, trinary, and even quarternary systems, Alpha Centauri A has companions—two of them—and they both orbit at relatively close range.

The outermost of the two companions currently lies between the sun and Alpha Centauri A and, because it is nearer to our solar system, has been named Proxima Centauri. This star is only a fraction the size of our sun, is some 20,000 times dimmer, and has become known to some astronomers as "the Cinderella star," traveling alone in such a wide-flung orbit that her light would not even cast a nighttime shadow on a planet circling Alpha Centauri A. The second star, called Alpha Centauri B, is 15 percent less massive than the sun, has a lower surface temperature, and will continue fusing hydrogen long after our sun and Alpha Centauri A have swollen to red giantism. The two stars circle around a common gravitational center, making one complete circuit every eighty years.

Until the *Pioneer* and *Voyager* spacecraft drove home the message that gas giants like Jupiter and Saturn are actually minor suns (they

The Horsehead nebula in Orion is perhaps the most dramatic example of obscuration produced by interstellar gas and dust. The Horsehead is about 1,300 light years from Earth. It appears dark becaue there are no stars suitably placed to excite the particles, as in the case of background gas. *Courtesy of Hale Observatories.*

The Pleiades, located about 400 light years from Earth in the constellation Taurus, is a cluster of stars born 60 million years ago, while the last of the dinosaurs roamed across Wyoming and Montana. The bright halos around the stars are lingering remnants of the cloud from which they were formed. *Courtesy of Hale Observatories.*

never accumulated enough mass to burn brightly as second and third stars in our solar system), astronomers generally agreed that one or both members of a close binary system might have planets in stable orbits, but that the chance was not very great. That chance is the basis of new models for binary systems proposed by Robert and Betty Harrington of the U.S. Naval Observatory. From computer simulations of the orbits of hypothetical sister stars and their associated planets, they have concluded that a planet's orbit will remain stable as long as the second sun (assuming a sun of approximately one solar mass) never approaches within a radius of 3.5 times the distance of the planet from its nearer star (the one around which it orbits).

Alpha Centauri A and B are separated by a minimum distance of 11 astronomical units (an astronomical unit is equivalent to 93 million miles, the mean distance between the Earth and the sun). If Alpha Centauri B were to be inserted into our own solar system at that same distance, it would lie between the orbits of Saturn and Uranus. Both planets would be flung immediately out of the solar system. Farther out, at a mean distance of 34.79 astronomical units from the sun, Neptune, Pluto, and Charon would suffer the same fate. Jupiter and its moons, 5.20 astronomical units from the sun, would orbit like drunkards, but Mars, 1.52 astronomical units away, would have a stable orbit, as would Earth, Venus, and Mercury. From Earth, the disk of Alpha Centauri B would appear several times smaller than a green pea held out at arm's distance, and it would shine 100 times brighter than the full moon. Thus, a planet in the warm, habitable zone of Alpha Centauri A, comparable to the orbit of Earth, would be quite unaffected by the presence of the second star.

If, instead of inserting Alpha Centauri B suddenly between the or-

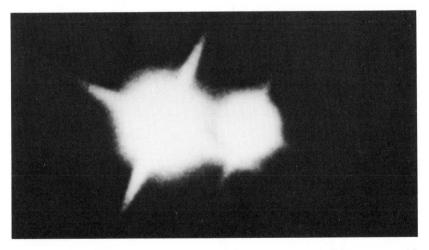

Alpha Centauri A and B are members of a multiple star system some 4.34 light years away. The brighter star is very near to our sun in type, size, and luminosity. If there were observers on a planet circling one member of the pair, they would see our sun as a star of 1st magnitude near the Cassiopeia-Perseus border, a few degrees northeast of the Perseus double cluster. No telescope on Earth would be able to detect light reflected from the planet Jupiter, or even to resolve the sun as a disk. *Courtesy of the Carter National Observatory, New Zealand.*

bits of Saturn and Uranus, we allow ourselves to imagine the star forming *with* our sun, then Saturn, Uranus, and their satellites, rather than being cast out of the solar system, will form as planets around the second sun—a solar system within a solar system.

Jupiter almost qualifies as a sister star (albeit a very small one) and, although it resides much closer to our sun than Alpha Centauri A and B are to each other, it nevertheless managed to acquire no fewer than fourteen satellites, each of them a world in its own right. But Jupiter and the sun seem to have created a no-man's-land between them, a place where the orbits of some satellites could overlap, bringing them into frequent contact with each other. The result is a cosmic demolition derby that virtually forbids planet formation at a range of 2.77 astronomical units from the sun. Seen from afar, this *shatter zone* resembles a faint ring around the sun, inserted between the orbits of Mars and Jupiter. Almost certainly, Alpha Centauri A and B share a shatter zone. From Alpha Centauti A, it would be located at a distance comparable to the orbit of Jupiter, a safe distance from the habitable zones of both stars, where planets with continents and oceans of liquid water may form.

In a single-star system like ours, it is unlikely that two warm, Earth-like planets would develop (even one is perhaps stretching the odds a bit far). But in a system like Alpha Centauri there are two habitable zones—two chances, one around each star; and there seems to be no reason (other than "bad luck") why Earth should not have an approximate likeness of itself circling at least one member of the pair. Hence, as we begin to search for oncoming laser beams and 21-centimeter (8.25-inch) wavelength radiation* in the hope that somebody out there may be trying to tell us something, multiple star systems like Alpha Centauri are likely to be the first places we should aim our equipment.

---

* Hydrogen atoms in cold space sometimes undergo a spontaneous change in configuration that emits a photon in the 21-cm wavelength. In a universe laced with hydrogen atoms, the 21-cm wavelength is everywhere, so it is of primary concern to those studying the properties of deep space. Exobiologists hoping to catch snatches of conversation between the stars are working from the hypothesis that distant civilizations will, like ourselves, have radio-telescopes designed to receive 21-cm wavelength radiation. That wavelength would seem to be a logical starting point in our search for deliberate signals. If our astronomers ever detect a stream of 21-cm radiation that contains few, if any, other wavelengths, and if the source winks on and off or flutters in a manner that is not truly regular, yet not entirely random, they will become suspicious.

5
Touchstones

Meteorites are busted pieces of stained glass windows—windows that let you look back in time.

Gerald Wasserburg

What seest thou else
In the dark backward and abysm of time?

William Shakespeare

Down there on Earth, long before the sun had reached the Ganges below them, the peaks of the Himalayas began blazing in the dawn, brilliant islands rising out of a sea of darkness, rolling into the line of daylight that had come sweeping across the Pacific and now bisected the South China Sea. Somewhere over Australia, an ancient rock mass slid into the upper atmosphere. It bounced, danced, and leaped down the air, trailing fire and sonic booms as it fell, then exploded over the town of Murchison, shaking buildings, rattling windows, and "scaring the daylights" out of residents. From the resulting dust cloud rained incandescent fragments that left a "footprint" 11 kilometers long by 3 kilometers wide (approximately 7 by 2 miles). One family claimed to have heard the thud and clatter of a heavy stone on their tin roof; and for several days thereafter, residents and scientists recovered "funny-looking shards of grayish matter" from fields, roadsides, and rooftops. The pieces resembled dried, almost charcoal-colored clay, and crumbled with similar ease.

Upon closer examination, their matrix appeared to be studded with tiny glass spheres. When these were sectioned and viewed under a microscope, layers of material, not unlike those distinctive patterns recognized in pearls, became visible. The small green spheres, called condrules, contained large amounts of magnesium and sometimes iron. Further analysis revealed unexpected traces of water (as high as 10 percent by weight) locked inside the stony fragments. On the morning of September 28, 1969, the twentieth specimen then known of that most puzzling and sought after of all meteorite types, the carbonaceous chondrite (named after the chondrules it contains), had arrived.

Only a few months earlier, men from the planet Earth had first set foot upon the moon. Among the treasures they sought were car-

A photomicrograph of a fragment from the Murchison meteorite shows light-colored chondrules immersed in a darker groundmass that is relatively rich in carbon. The width of the field is approximately 5 millimeters. *Photo by C. R. Pellegrino and J. A. Stoff.*

bonaceous chondrites, valued for the clues they offer about the birth stages of the solar system and even the origin of life. (At that time, the whole world's supply of carbonaceous chondrites was small enough to be contained in an average-sized desk drawer.) Six manned Apollo missions and three Soviet robots brought back 360 kilograms (approximately 800 pounds) of rock, one or two kilograms of which consisted of carbonaceous dust mixed in with the lunar soil. In one of those "jokes" that nature delights in playing on us, over 900 kilograms (2,000 pounds) of carbonaceous chondrite material landed on Earth within months of the first Apollo expedition; a second giant carbonaceous chondrite lit the skies over northern Mexico and showered a small hamlet named Allende, even as scientists in California and New York eagerly awaited their allotments of the first lunar samples.

Nearly three years after its arrival, scientists at NASA's Ames Research Center in California confirmed the presence of complex, ring-shaped carbon compounds (sometimes incorporating nitrogen and oxygen), seventeen different fatty acids, and eighteen amino acids in fragments of the Murchison meteorite. Of particular interest are the amino acids because, woven properly together, they comprise the very foundations of cellular life. They are relatively simple organic compounds composed of hydrogen, carbon, oxygen, and nitrogen, with the occasional introduction of sulfur and nonmetallic elements (halogens) such as flourine, chlorine, iodine, bromine, and astatine. They are characterized by having at least one amine group (NH_2) and at least one carboxylic acid group (COOH) and are the bricks from which protein molecules are built.

But one very important question soon arose: Were these substances truly native to the meteorite, or did the meteorite, upon penetrating the atmosphere and scattering its pieces in vegetable gardens and children's sandboxes, begin to "breathe in" earthly contaminants? After all, a mere fingerprint on its surface—or a cough or sneeze from a person collecting the pieces—would have contributed most of the common amino acids known here on Earth.

During the three-year investigation that followed its arrival, the Murchison meteorite was examined and compared closely with another carbonaceous chondrite that had fallen near Murray, Kentucky, nineteen years earlier. The results were impressively similar. Of the eighteen amino acids detected in the two meteorites, six of them

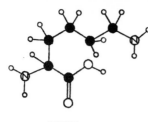

LYSINE

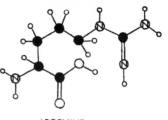

ARGENINE

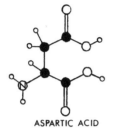

ASPARTIC ACID

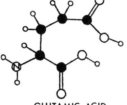

GLUTAMIC ACID

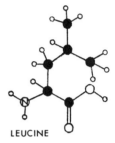

LEUCINE

SERINE

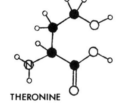

THERONINE

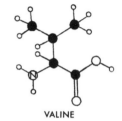

VALINE

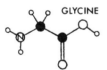

GLYCINE

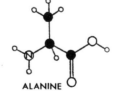

ALANINE

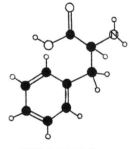

PHENYLALANINE

○ HYDROGEN

● CARBON

Ⓝ NₗTROGEN

○ OXYGEN

Some amino acids found in carbonaceous meteorites.

Amino acids in hydrolyzed extracts of the Murchison and Murray meteorites.

Peak	Amino acid	Murchison		Murray	
		Amount (μg/g)	Ratio (relative to glycine)	Amount (μg/g)	Ratio (relative to glycine)
Amino acids found in proteins					
11	Aspartic acid	1.7	0.3	1.6	0.5
14	Glutamic acid	3.1	0.5	1.6	0.5
15	Proline	1.3	0.2	0.4	0.1
17	Glycine	6.1	1.0	3.0	1.0
18	Alanine	3.5	0.6	1.3	0.4
21	Valine/isovaline	1.6	0.3	0.9	0.3
Amino acids not found in proteins					
19	α-Aminoisobutyric acid	2.5	0.4	11.4	3.8
20	α-Amino-n-butyric acid	1.1	0.2	0.5	0.2
32	β-Alanine	0.4	0.1	1.2	0.4
33	β-Aminoisobutyric acid	0.7	0.1	0.3	0.1

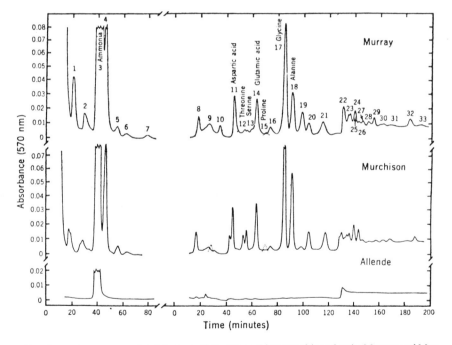

Gas chromatograms reveal strikingly similar amino acid compositions for the Murray and Murchison carbonaceous meteorities. The Allende meteorite is shown to be essentially devoid of amino acids. Glycine, the simplest amino acid, is seen in greatest abundance. *Reprinted from Cronin and Moore, 1975. Copyright 1975 by the American Association for the Advancement of Science.*

(glycine, alanine, valine, aspartic acid, glutamic acid, and proline) are prominent in earthly proteins. The remaining twelve (isovaline, a-aminoisobutyric acid, N-methylalanine, a-aminobutyric acid, N-methylglycine, N-ethylglycine, norvaline, B-aminoisobutyric acid, B-aminobutyric acid, pipecolic acid, B-alanine, and y-aminobutyric acid) are related but are seldom if ever associated with the living tissues of terrestrial plants and animals. This anomaly by itself explodes P. B. Hamilton's claim that "what appears to be the pitter-patter of heavenly feet is probably instead the print of an earthly thumb," and clears the path for speculation about how and where these substances were manufactured.

The meteorites seem to have formed during an age when the gas and dust of the solar nebula was falling together into little gravitational bodies that became celestial vacuum cleaners, ever increasing in girth as they continued to sweep up debris in their path. Some, like our own Earth, accumulated great mass. Their interiors began to heat up. Gases, steam, and vaporized rock held fast to their shifting skin. The primordial atmospheres were born.

The sweeping-up process is still taking place today, although at a much slower rate than in the past. There is simply not a great deal of "dust" left in the solar system. Nevertheless, the Earth is gaining weight on the order of about 100,000 kilograms (approximately 50,000 pounds) a day. Tens of kilometers above our heads, uncountable marble, sand grain, and corpuscle-sized particles plunge into the atmosphere, scratching fire across the sky. Most of them are vaporized before they ever reach the ground, and a few of them are flecks of iron, the iron that was forged deep inside at least one large star that was not our sun. The majority of this iron, however, was remelted during the formation of the solar system and resided for at least several million years inside county-, state-, or even continent-sized accumulations of rock that were split open and ground down by successive encounters with other rocks. A very small amount of interstellar iron might have escaped being swept up by larger bodies and thus remained unchanged since the day it was coughed up by an aging star. You can collect small quantities of iron vapor right in your own back yard by leaving clean trays or pie platters out in the rain and then using a magnet sheathed in a plastic sandwich bag to skim the bottoms of the trays. Under a microscope, the meteoritic iron will look like tiny

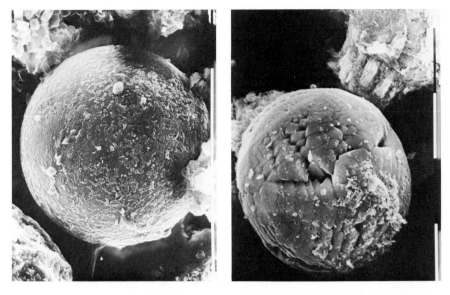

Meteorites plunging into the atmosphere add upward of 100,000 kg of weight to the Earth every day. Few of them ever penetrate through to the ground, and the smoke of their burning mingles with pollen grains and wind-blown dust to become seeds around which water vapor may condense. Some of the cosmic dust accumulating in clouds is magnetic, which facilitates its collection. The nickel-iron microspheres shown in these scanning electron micrographs were gathered from a water trap in the senior author's back yard only minutes after a thunder storm. The larger spherule has a diameter of approximately 100 μ. The smaller, which contains sulfur, measures approximately 30 μ across. *Photos by C. R. Pellegrino and K. Goldie.*

metallic globes. These are the smoke of ancient nuggets of metal that flashed and burned and flared as they dove into our atmosphere at several kilometers per second.

Whether the result of a shatter zone created by the sun and Jupiter or merely a collection of discarded planetary scraps left hanging about the sun, a belt of solar driftwood—the asteroids—spreads wide between Mars and Jupiter. It is from this belt that most meteorites seem to originate.

A typical asteroid field probably bears little resemblance to the one depicted in the world-famous *Empire Strikes Back*. With all due apologies to Artoo (as much as we love him), the asteroids do not lie shoulder to shoulder. In fact, two *Pioneer* and two *Voyager* spacecraft have already flown straight through the asteroid belt without crashing into so much as a single pebble; and NASA scientists

Taenite crystals in a cut, polished, and acid-etched nickel-iron meteorite. Detailed chemical analyses suggest that the interlocking metallic crystals formed very slowly, having solidified from a molten state in an environment that cooled by as litle as 1°C every million years. *Courtesy of Robert A. Oriti Collection, Griffith Observatory.*

estimate that up to 200 more spacecraft would have to follow before "a serious fender-bender" would result. Standing on the surface of Psyche, an iron nugget some 250 kilometers (155 miles) across, your nearest neighbor of any appreciable size would be a distant, wandering point of light. More than 4,000 asteroids are currently known; and those are the ones bright enough to be seen through telescopes from a distance of 265 million kilometers (approximately 165 million miles). The majority of these minor planets, especially those orbiting at the well-defined, ring-like inner edge of the belt, are strongly concentrated in the plane of the solar system (in which the orbits of most of the planets, their satellites, and the sun's equator lie). As we look farther out across the belt, toward Jupiter, the orbits become increas-

The twelve largest asteroids.

NAME	DIAMETER (KILOMETERS)	ALBEDO (PERCENT)	SURFACE TYPE
Ceres	1000	5.4	carbonaceous
Pallas	605	7.4	peculiar carbon
Vesta	530	22.9	eucritic
Hygeia	450	4.1	peculiar carbon
Euphrosyne	370	3.0	carbonaceous
Interamnia	345	3.3	carbonaceous
Davida	320	3.7	carbonaceous
Cybele	305	2.2	carbonaceous
Europa	290	3.5	carbonaceous
Patientia	275	2.6	carbonaceous
Eunomia	275	15.5	siliceous
Psyche	250	9.3	metallic iron

ingly eccentric until, at the outer edge, the asteroids are widely scattered above and below the solar-system plane.

During the 1970s, detailed computer analyses of asteroid orbits suggested that the belt is in a highly fragmented state, having originated as a family of at least fifty minor planets with diameters ranging generally between 100 and 1,000 kilometers (approximately 60 to 620 miles). These are believed to have accreted during the birth stages of the solar system, but would have begun almost immediately to suffer mutual collisions, thereby cracking, rupturing, and spewing their contents. A few of the larger, spheroidal asteroids, like Ceres, which has a diameter of approximately 1,000 kilometers, might have survived relatively intact. The current model for a body like Ceres suggests an early period of internal melting generated over the volume of the asteroid by radioactive elements—a lot of them—fresh and hot from a supernova explosion.* Heavy elements, like iron and platinum, would

---

* Gerald Wasserburg and his team at California Institute of Technology's Lunatic Asylum (yes, that's what they call themselves) have provided answers to one of Harold C. Urey's old puzzlements: "How were the small planets melted?" In 1977 the team became very excited about the discovery of large quantities of magnesium 26 in a piece of the Allende meteorite, and with good reason. Magnesium 26 is the daughter decay product of aluminum 26. Aluminum 26 differs from aluminum 27 in having one less neutron and, unlike the aluminum we are more familiar with (27), is unstable (radioactive). Compared with the age of the solar system, aluminum 26 has a very short half life, only 740,000 years, during which 1,000 atoms of the isotope will become 500 atoms of aluminum 26 and 500 atoms of magnesium 26 (the term isotope defines any of two or more forms of the same element, in this case aluminum, having the

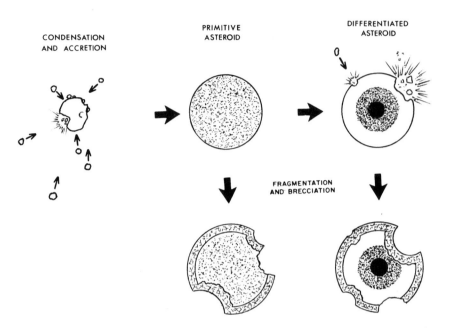

An abbreviated view of the formation of parent bodies from which most meteorites seem to be derived. Planetisimals that formed in the asteroid belt are on the order of 100 kilometers in diameter. Melting and differentiation is believed to have occurred in objects of this size. *By permission, Laura L. "The Asteroids: accretion, differentiation, fragmentation, and irradiation," in ASTEROIDS, T. Gehrels, Editor, Tucson: University of Arizona Press, Copyright. Illustration by C. R. Pellegrino.*

have sunk toward the center, leading to the formation of a metallic core overlaid with stony iron material encased in a thick outer shell of silicates mixed with varying concentrations of ice, salt, and carbonaceous deposits. The hard, metal-rich cores of such bodies do not fragment very easily; and some planetary geologists have suggested

---

same number of protons in the nucleus, or the same atomic number, but different numbers of neutrons in the nucleus, or different atomic weights). After 1.5 million years, only 250 atoms of aluminum 26 will remain; and 5 million years later, the element will be practically extinct, almost wholly decayed into magnesium 26.

The significance of accumulations of magnesium 26 in the Allende meteorite lies in their proof that aluminum 26 did indeed exist, enough of it, in fact, to have generated rapid heating as it decayed inside the meteorite parent body. Perhaps more significant is that vast quantities of aluminum 26 would have had to be freshly manufactured in a supernova, then injected rapidly into the presolar nebula just prior to or during its collapse. The Asylum has also identified the daughter decay products of a palladium isotope (also thought to be extinct) in the Allende meteorite, suggesting that there is a bonanza of ancient, short-lived, and very hot isotopes yet to be found.

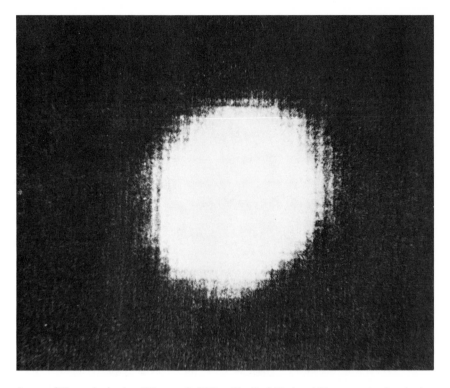

Image of Vesta obtained on February 3, 1977 at Kitt Peak National Observatory using the 4-m telescope and a very short exposure time. The short exposure time minimized the image-degrading effects of atmospheric turbulence. Using an image intensifier, a speckle pattern of Vesta was reconstructed. The asteroid, with a diameter of 530 kilometers (330 miles), has a spheroidal shape. For objects in this size range, shape appears to be determined largely by gravity, which is sufficient to pull the rock mass together into a sphere. For objects with diameters less than 200 kilometers, cratering seems to be the dominating shaping force, and such bodies frequently resemble broken teeth. The asteroid disk shown here is 0.470 arc seconds in diameter, which corresponds to the diameter of a pinhead seen at 500 meters. *Courtesy of Kitt Peak National Observatory.*

that several reddish asteroids in the 40 to 200 kilometer size range (approximately 25 to 125 miles) are the stony iron interiors of partially remelted, differentiated asteroids that have had their outer layers blasted off in collisions.

The whole asteroid belt is agitated continually by the gravitational influence of Jupiter. Like a gardener, the giant planet has dug trenches in the field, concentric gaps that resemble the divisions in

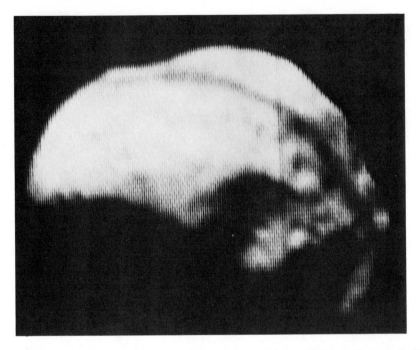

Voyager I image of Saturn's eleventh moon, a trailing, co-orbital satellite located between the F and G rings. The photograph was taken on November 12, 1980, at a distance of 177,000 kilometers (110,000 miles). The satellite with dimensions of 135 × 70 kilometers (83 × 43 miles) and low albedo is representative of a moderately large asteroid. *Provided through the courtesy of National Aeronautics and Space Administration, California Institute of Technology, Jet Propulsion Laboratories.*

Saturn's rings and occur at fractions of Jupiter's 11.9 year orbital period. Like the gardener, Jupiter weeds its field, occasionally yanking a pebble, a boulder, or a flying mountain loose and dropping it toward the sun. Because of this, about 5 percent of the known asteroids travel in eccentric ellipses, like short-period comets. Several of these pass close to the Earth and, according to recent figures provided by Princeton University astronomer Scott Dunbar, small asteroids could be trapped along the Earth's orbit (the implications for mining and construction in space are clear, and the space telescope will soon be used to determine whether or not these objects exist).

Each day, little crumbs from the asteroid belt, and elsewhere, plunge into our atmosphere; and one or two of them manage to penetrate through to the ground (every few hundred-thousand years or so we get the whole cake: see chapter 11). The presence of highly complex organic molecules in some of these meteorites opens up a hornet's nest of problems, not the least of which is that amino acids, fatty acids, alcohols, phenols, sugars, purines, and pyrimidines seem to have no business being out there in the first place. If they are native to the meteorites, then we are faced with a perplexing fact: These carbon compounds were somehow lifted, against entropy, to a highly ordered state from vast numbers of random, dissociated, inanimate atoms that were gathered up and arranged in their present condition of seemingly improbable symmetry. Given only the extreme temperatures, damaging radiation, and near emptiness of outer space, it is not likely that this kind of clustering could have proceeded on objects so small as stones, boulders, or even asteroids (nor that it should be reproduced so agreeably among two samples falling on opposite sides of the world 19 years apart).

Detailed comparisons with earthly tissues seem to sharpen the contrasts between terrestrial biochemistry and the species of molecular ornamentation residing inside carbonaceous chondrites. That the history of these compounds differs from our own is underscored by important eccentricities in their design.

Most molecular biologists agree that when the Earth was still in its infancy, when its vapors had condensed into newly formed seas and its shroud of air contained few destructive oxidizing agents, the first organic acids were probably assembled in two very distinct varieties. Alanine, for example, probably occurred as mirror images of itself, much in the same way as your right and left hands are mirror images, or *stereoenantiomers,* of each other. In those days before the dawn of living, self-replicating matter, both "right-handed" and "left-handed" amino acids might have drifted about the Precambrian seas in equal or near-equal quantities.

When living things finally did take over the Earth, the assembly of proteins was made possible only by the uptake of entirely right-handed or entirely left-handed amino acids. The geometry of long-chain carbon compounds does not permit random associations of both right-handed and left-handed components in their construction. On Earth, it was the left-handed variety that won acceptance. Hence, terrestrial proteins, whether they are derived from trees or mosquitos or men (except for a special class of single-celled organisms, which

MIRROR

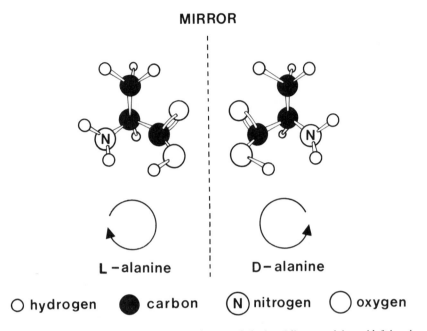

L −alanine   D− alanine

○ hydrogen   ● carbon   (N) nitrogen   ○ oxygen

Schematic illustration of L and D stereonantiomers of alanine. Like your right and left hands, neither molecule can be superimposed upon the other, in spite of their identical composition. They differ in the configuration of the four chemical groups around the central carbon atom: D-alanine has the NH_2 group attached to the left of the carbon atom and the COOH to the right, while the reverse is true for L-alanine. Arrows (*bottom*) indicate that L-alanine will rotate a beam of plane-polarized light to the left, whereas D-alanine will twist it to the right.

utilize some right-handed amino acids in their cell walls), are composed entirely of left-handed amino acids.

Using a beam of plane-polarized light, we can determine the right-handedness or left-handedness of a set of molecules. Almost all right-handed molecules will twist or rotate a plane of polarization to the right, whereas the left-handed variety will twist it to the left. When homogenous mixtures of amino acids from the Murray and Murchison meteorites were examined using gas chromatography* they

---

* The compounds were passed as vapor into a stream of helium and fed through nearly 50 meters of capillary tubing, where they separated and began to migrate at different speeds through a solvent coated on the inside of the tube. The rate of passage through the solvent was a function of each compound's unique physical properties. The separated compounds then emerged into a hydrogen flame and were ionized. The resulting surges of electrically charged atoms could then be measured as changes in current across a detector. Translated onto a chart, the changes in current were recorded as a series of peaks corresponding to individual compounds.

were found to be optically inactive. They would therefore fail to rotate a plane of polarized light. Each stereoenantiomer of a given amino acid was present in nearly equal quantities. These findings are reminiscent of ratios presumed to have existed in Precambrian seas prior to the emergence of cellular enzyme activity, and they strongly suggest an origin not in the biology of cells, but in the chemistry of atoms.

The nature of meteoritic amino acids differs from those in your fingertips, to be sure. Equal distributions of both left- and right-handed molecular configurations would seem to cast serious doubts on the feasibility of their ever having been generated by any kind of cellular activity or by life as we know it. Nevertheless, comparison of the Murchison chondrites with other carbonaceous chondrite meteorites occasionally leads to points of confusion. A meteorite that fell in Orgueil, France, in 1864 and a 1938 fall in Ivuna, Tanganyika, both contain greater traces of left-handed than right-handed amino acids. Because meteorite core samples are deficient in such common earthly contaminants as serine and theronine, the amino acids appear to be indigenous but for unknown reasons are optically active.

We can already provide a good explanation for discrepancies in ratios of amino acid among carbonaceous chondrites. Given irradiation by light, heat, X-ray, or other energy sources, amino acids can interconvert from one form to another. For example, a solitary left-handed molecule of alanine, impelled by a constant input of energy, would eventually flip over to a right-handed configuration. An entire vial of left-handed alanine exposed to the radiations of the sun would, given enough time, undergo total interconversion. One should not, however, expect to recover a vial filled only with right-handed molecules since, once produced, they are as likely to flip over to the left-handed variety as left-handed molecules are to become right-handed. The situation is analogous to laying a million pennies heads-up (to represent the left-handed molecules) in a large tray; by randomly tossing handfuls of them into the air—our application of energy—more and more of the pennies would land heads-*down,* until the distribution of heads and tails was nearly equal. Probabilities being what they are, from this point on we would always expect to find about the same number of heads and tails no matter how many more handfuls were tossed.

Thus, a vial of pure left-handed alanine suspended in space and irradiated (but not fried) for a million years or so would ultimately turn up as an optically inactive mixture of left-handed and right-handed molecules (optically inactive mixtures, which do not rotate a plane of polarized light, are said to be racemic), in spite of its initially pure form.

The Murray and Murchison meteorites are among the lightest and least densely packed of the nearly forty carbonaceous chondrites known today (the recent discovery of remarkably well-preserved meteorites on the Antarctic ice sheet has effectively doubled the pre-1969 number of available specimens). If, during their long passage through the solar system, they were ever part of large asteroidal bodies, then surely they resided on or very near the surface. Consequently, their contents were left naked to the raw energies of space, and amino acids recovered from these meteorites are presumed to have undergone many "flips of the coin"—they have become utterly random. A meteorite originating in the depths of a parent body, on the other hand, would have received more adequate shielding against such energy.

The Ivuna and Orgueil specimens reveal compression of their matrix, implying the operation of mild gravitational forces exerted by overlying rock in their respective parent bodies. Mixtures of amino acids extracted from these meteorites deviate sharply from the half-and-half composition of lighter specimens (which include the Murray and Murchison meteorites). Skewness among the denser carbonaceous chondrites infers an initial sample consisting largely or entirely of left-handed amino acids.

The reason for the predominance of left-handed rather than right-handed amino acids as protein constituents on Earth is unclear. It has been suggested in the past that some random event in the early Precambrian seas led to the preferential selection of left-handed amino acids, almost as though biological evolution had a choice of building proteins from either stereoenantiomer and somebody flipped a coin to decide the winner.

Astrophysicists are fond of pointing out that "God does not play dice with the universe." (Black-hole theorist Stephen W. Hawking has improved upon this phrase with what he calls his *principle of ignorance:* "God not only plays with dice, He sometimes throws them where they can't be seen".) Contemplating a Precambrian lake that has all sorts of amino acids and alcohols and sugars and ring-shaped organic compounds, it becomes tempting for biologists to remark, "God does not flip coins." (Yes, we know, when will scientists stop telling God what to do?) The truth of the matter is that it becomes very difficult to imagine the same accident being repeated over the entire volume of an ocean or a lake or even a puddle. Stephen C. Bondy and Marilyn E. Harrington of the University of Colorado Medical Center have shown that the selection of left-handed amino acids might have been determined by more than mere chance. They demonstrated, for example, that two amino acids (L-leucine and L-aspartate), which are common in earthly proteins, are selectively adsorbed onto bentonite (a type of clay), while their biologically uncommon right-handed counterparts tend to remain in solution. This suggests that left-handed amino acids had some inherent advantage over right-handed amino acids during early evolution; and it certainly complicates an interpretation of the relative abundance of right-handed amino acids in some carbonaceous chondrites.

Although the origin of meteoritic organic compounds is still a subject for speculation—and sometimes active debate—most planetary geologists and organic chemists are in agreement that they were contained in the meteorites prior to any contact with our atmosphere. Most will also agree that we are probably viewing the products of a naturally occurring chemical evolution that was frozen in midstride long before it had any chance of developing into living cells. If we assume the *least* glamorous hypothesis, then the first steps in the direction of life were taken elsewhere in our solar system, perhaps in several places, and have come to be preserved or fossilized in carbonaceous chondrites.

These celestial vagrants offer the alluring possibility that the universe is not such a lonely place in which to live. Clouds of formaldehyde spread throughout the arms of the galaxy seem to exemplify the trend: Wherever hydrogen, carbon, nitrogen, oxygen, and a few heavier elements lie scattered and heated at the right temperature, it is a fair bet that they will coalesce into compounds of higher order. That we are here is proof enough that such reactions can and sometimes do occur.

Note: For an update on meteorite D/L amino acid ratios, readers are referred to M.H. Engel and B. Nagy's report in the April 29, 1982 issue of *Nature.*

6
On Probability and Possibility

They couldn't hit an elephant at this dist. . . .

General John Sedgwick
(the last words of)

Charles Darwin saw at the cradle of life a *warm little pond.* "It is often said," he wrote to a friend in 1871,

> that all the conditions for the first production of a living organism are now present, which could ever have been present. But if (and oh what a big if) we could conceive in some warm little pond, with all sorts of ammonia and phosphoric salts, light, heat, electricity, etc., present, that a protein compound was chemically formed ready to undergo still more complex changes, at the present day such matter would be instantly devoured, or absorbed, which would not have been the case before living creatures were formed.

More than three-quarters of a century later at the University of Chicago, Stanley L. Miller and Harold C. Urey took sterilized water, free of both living organisms and their residues, added an atmosphere of hydrogen, ammonia, and methane, then subjected the mixture to continuous electrical discharge in a closed container for a week. During that week, carbon, hydrogen, nitrogen, and oxygen bonded to form simple amino acids. These compounds changed forever our vision of the origin of proteins and of life on Earth as an "accident" so improbable as to be a miracle that happened only once in the entire universe.

A particularly dramatic example of the ease with which the carbon atom bonds to produce compounds of higher organization was demonstrated during the Second World War. For years the Germans had been synthesizing hydrocarbon fuels on a commercial scale. Using burning rubbish as a heat source, mixtures of simple gases like methane were passed at high temperature over metallic ore catalysts (which accelerated the formation of chemical bonds) in closed pressure-cooker-like containers. (A variation on this process was explored by American industry from 1946 through 1952, but was determined, during the days of cheap oil from the Middle East, to be "not commercially viable".) The process did, however, have its shortcomings, primarily because of the production of unwanted by-products; these included amino acids, sugar precursors, nucleic acid bases, and fatty acids. Had it occurred to the German engineers that they were possibly simulating reactions between lava flows and a primitive terrestrial atmosphere, they might have gone to Sweden to claim their Nobel prize in chemistry.

Biology is the production of order from chaos. And it seems that the carbon atom, impelled by just a little energy, is a most splendid organizer. But it is an enormous jump from ordered molecules like amino acids to functional proteins.

Let us consider, for example, the insulin molecule, a relatively simple protein consisting of twenty different amino acids strung together in a particular configuration fifty amino acids long. The probability of finding one of the twenty types of amino acids at a certain position on the molecule is one chance in twenty. The probability of finding that amino acid and a specific neighbor joined together on the molecule is 20^{-2}, or one chance in 400; and the chance of finding three amino acids linked together in some particular fashion is 20^{-3}, or one in 8,000. For fifty amino acids, the probability is 20^{-50}, which is pushing the limits of possibility.

Take a vat big enough to contain an elephant. No, let's think of something bigger—a world! Take a whole world covered in a kilometer-deep sea of amino acid soup. Now, stir the sea. Pump in solar radiation so that the amino acids can snap together randomly and fly apart and snap together again; and let this go on uninterrupted

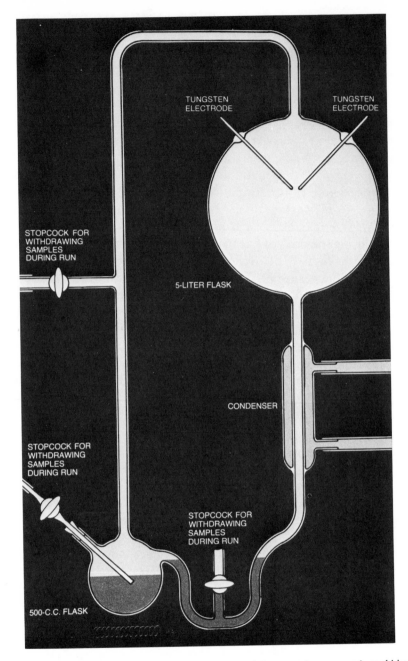

The Miller-Urey spark discharge apparatus demonstrated that organic compounds could have arisen spontaneously on a lifeless Earth through the input of energy. Water in the bottom flask was boiled to drive gases into the spark discharge chamber. The vapors were then condensed and became concentrated in solution at the bottom of the apparatus. *Courtesy of Scientific American.*

for a million years or so. But don't bet more than a year's subscription to *Time* that even once, for a single second, will a molecule of insulin be produced. Even a small protein like insulin is a structure of such gigantic improbability (one chance in 10^{-80}, which is a figure exceeding the estimated total of electrons in the universe) that your unguided efforts would probably fail to bring about its formation, even given all the galaxies to experiment with for a billion years.

But we *have* insulin in our bodies, and more. We have impossible proteins that are knitted together to form neurons, and neurons that become columns and networks arranged in modules in the cerebral cortex. And we have eyes, and awareness. Insulin and brain proteins are not produced by random, unguided nature, but are constructed from blueprints inherited from our ancestors. Track back far enough in time and you will encounter single-celled forebears whose blueprints (molecules of DNA) did not call for the construction of insulin and brain proteins. Track back farther still and what do you think you will find?

Our best guess is that the Earth's first inhabitants were hollow droplets of simple proteins formed by random aggregation; we call them protobionts or protocells. There would have been billions of them forming and dissolving in the primeval seas almost every day, many of them capable of sustaining some primitive metabolic activities, most of them doomed to being diluted out of existence, and no two of them exactly alike.

The Protocell era (about 3.6 to 4.0 billion years ago), from which simple organic compounds emerged as living cells complete with genetic machinery, left few traces of itself in the fossil record. Protocells, as a rule, were not frequently preserved as fossils and, even if they were, more than 3.5 billion years of earthquake, wind, and rain have erased them so utterly that the first few chapters in the history of life are all but missing. An accurate reconstruction of what preceded the development of a genetic apparatus will have to await comparisons with life (or better yet with its birth stages) elsewhere in our neighborhood of stars. In the meantime, we must turn to laboratory models, hoping to reproduce the physical and chemical setting of a world we know very little about.

Two such models have come from the laboratories of Sidney W. Fox at the University of Miami and Alexander I. Oparin at the A.N.

3.50 BILLION YEARS AGO	FOSSIL CELLS; FORMATION OF THE LUNAR MARIA.
3.76 BILLION YEARS AGO	PROBABLE PROTOCELL FOSSILS (FROM GREENLAND).
≤4.00 BILLION YEARS AGO	PROTOCELL ERA BEGINS.
4.45 BILLION YEARS AGO	FORMATION OF THE EARTH'S CRUST.
4.60 BILLION YEARS AGO	COLLAPSE OF THE PRESOLAR NEBULA.

The first billion years of Earth history.

Bakh Institute for Biochemistry in Moscow. From these models we have learned that as long as you do not start calling out "I want an alanine here and a valine right behind it and a guanine over there, et cetera," and are willing to accept randomly assembled proteins as they come, then there is no problem with probability and the generation of early proteins. Fox has demonstrated that amino acids mixed in water, then poured over hot volcanic rock and washed off with more water will aggregate spontaneously into hollow, proteinaceous spheres 10 to 20 microns (10,000 microns = 1 centimeter) in diameter. Under the right conditions, the microspheres will grow, absorbing the dissolved amino acids onto their surfaces, and will bud and fission in a manner hauntingly reminiscent of bacteria or algae. These giant molecules are also catalytically powerful. For example, they can promote the decomposition of glucose, or the hydrolysis (whereby a compound is split into smaller components by the uptake of hydrogen and oxygen) of esters (which are formed by the joining of an alcohol and an acid with the release of a molecule of water) into alcohols and acids.

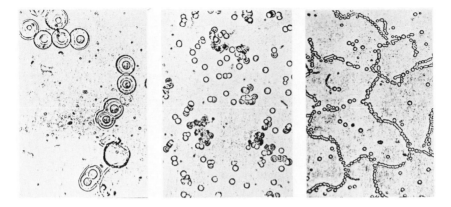

The polymer-rich droplets shown here were produced by University of Miami molecular biologist Sidney W. Fox using mixtures of amino acids dispersed in water and then washed over hot volcanic rocks. Under suitable conditions, the microspheres will grow and eventually bud. They display a two-layer membrane suggestive of that in bacteria (*left*) and frequently form associations reminiscent of algae (*right*). All microspheres shown here are approximately 10 microns in diameter. *Courtesy of S. W. Fox and the New York Academy of Science.*

Oparin has carried this one step farther. His team discovered early in its studies that almost any combination of biological polymers (large molecules formed by the addition of many smaller molecules, such as protein, carbohydrates, or DNA) mixed in water tended to separate out of solution as colloidal droplets; but these droplets also tended to be unstable, settling to the bottom and quickly deteriorating into a hopeless, sticky layer. The next obvious step was to determine whether or not conditions existed that would stabilize suspensions of coacervate droplets (the name given to Oparin microstructures) for hours, days, or weeks at a time. The tantalizing conclusion was that the droplets could be easily stabilized if they were given a primitive metabolism.

Oparin found that when he added the enzyme phosphorylase (which is widely occurring in plant and animal tissues and, in the presence of a sugar phosphate, catalyzes its conversion into glycogen, also known as *animal starch*) to a solution containing coacervates built up from histone (a protein) and gum arabic (a polysaccharide), the enzyme became concentrated inside the droplets. If he then added glucose-1-phosphate, it diffused from the surrounding water into the

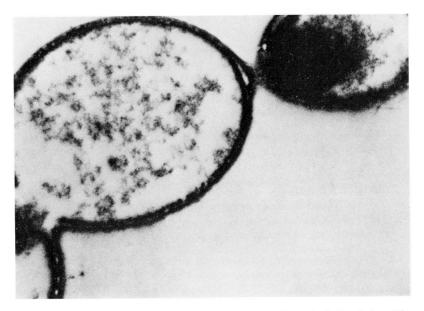

These coacervates were formed in the Moscow laboratory of Alexander I. Oparin by adding a mixture of protamine and polyadenylic acid to water. If provided with a primitive metabolism, the microscopic droplets will grow and divide in a manner hauntingly reminiscent of living cells. *Courtesy of Dr. A. I. Oparin.*

droplets and was polymerized—snapped together piece-by-piece into long molecules of starch—by the enzyme. Since gum arabic is itself a sugar polymer, the starch became part of the coacervate, adding to its thick membrane-like mantle, increasing the total volume of the droplet, and causing it to swell. Energy for continued polymerization came from breakage of the phosphate bond in glucose-1-phosphate. The phosphate, once released, diffused back out of the droplet as a "waste product."

Coacervate droplets, given a metabolism of this kind, began to grow, their walls thickening, until at last they broke up into several daughter droplets. Those that happened to receive molecules of phosphorylase enzyme continued to metabolise glucose-1-phosphate, growing as they did so and then dividing again. But the process slowed down with each successive episode of growth and division because the original supply of enzyme molecules became increasingly dilute. If there were some way for the coacervate droplets to synthesize more

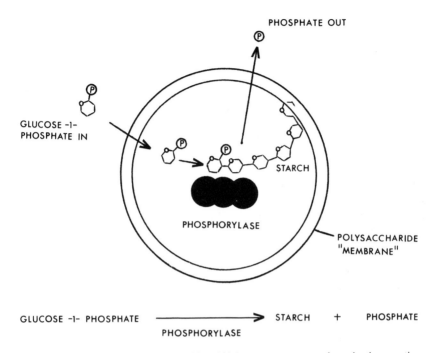

Stabilization of coacervate droplets is achieved if they can carry out polymerization reactions. The addition of phosphorylase enzyme to a solution containing coacervates enables them to polymerize glucose-1-phosphate to starch. The starch becomes concentrated in the wall and increases the volume of the droplet.

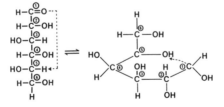

Carbohydrates are short carbon chains, usually from three to seven carbon atoms long. Each carbon in the chain, except one, carries a hydroxyl (OH) group. The remaining carbon carries a carboxyl group (an oxygen atom attached by a double bond). Like glucose, shown here, they can join head-to-tail to form ring compounds. Carbohydrates are oxidized as fuel substances by all cells, and they form the supporting tissues (cellulose) of plants. The numbers indicate positions of carbon atoms on the molecule.

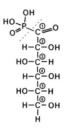

The structure of glucose-1-phosphate.

phosphorylase enzyme and pass the same catalytic abilities onto each daughter droplet, the coacervates would have become self-sustaining, almost immortal, almost alive. They could grow and multiply and nurture themselves for as long as a supply of glucose-1-phosphate remained available.

We would never want to make a gross claim that life in the Precambrian seas began from microscopic balls of histone and tree sap feeding on sugar. The Fox and Oparin microbodies are only analogies of a preliving chemical evolution, but, still, they are suggestive of a historical connection between it and us; and they provide clues about the behavior of randomly assembled proteins, the things from which insulin and brain tissue later evolved, the subject to which we shall now return.

Simplifying the probability picture (if only slightly), molecular biologists have learned that a particular enzyme function, the breakdown of glucose, for example, can be carried out not by one, but often by a variety of amino acid sequences. Only a small part of a chain of amino acids, generally located at a single place on a protein molecule, seems to characterize its function. This is known as the active catalytic site and, while the rest of the molecule may serve as a stabilizing agent or provide docking space and other services, it is, for

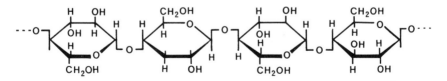

Polysaccharides, like the cellulose segment shown here, are formed by the end-to-end linkage of monosaccharides (in this case the carbohydrate glucose).

the most part, inert. Thus, insulin molecules extracted from the pancreas of a sheep, mouse, whale, or polar bear, though different in some aspects of structure and composition from human insulin, will be able to metabolise glucose and other carbohydrates in the human body. (Nowhere else in the universe is human insulin reproduced in every detail, but is does have look-alikes; just as airless moon-like worlds all look basically the same, yet no two have identical crater fields.)

A whole cell can be irradiated with X-rays until the proteins it manufactures begin to look like dwarfs, giants, and cripples. We can turn its genetic information into "scrambled eggs," yet the mixing of amino acid sequences in a specific protein molecule will not often inactivate or even significantly hinder its function. (This can be said of many single-celled organisms or even of such complex creatures as cockroaches, which function and survive in spite of the scrambling effects of moderate X-ray dosages; but in the case of birds and mammals, where portions of one protein frequently effect the synthesis and operation of other proteins, such scrambling can prove disastrous.)

Certainly the first "useful" proteins, those that by sheer chance appeared on or in floating bags of polymer and were able to induce polymerizations that added to the bulk of the droplet, contained as few as five or six amino acids which, arranged in some particular order almost anywhere on a protein molecule, prolonged the survival of the droplet. The activities of these amino acids would have progressed at a slow pace, and primitive enzymes would not have been very discriminating about what they bonded together or broke apart or when they did so. The survival potential of a protocell would be directly related to the complexity and effectiveness of its metabolism; and time, the destroyer, would see to it that most protocells and their descendents ran down and eventually fell apart, dispersing their contents for future reabsorpsion by other protocells. Those droplets possessing the ability to absorb molecules from their surroundings, and to capture energy and direct it toward the knitting together of small molecules into substances that could promote the survival not only of the droplets, but of their daughter droplets, probably became ancestors of the first true living things to populate our planet's seas. What was needed was an orderly mechanism, something like a team of carpenters and a set of blueprints to be passed on to each daughter droplet and guarantee that it was able to construct the same enzymes needed for all the reactions important to its parent's survival.

There are no adequate laboratory models for how genetic machinery involving a complex interrelationship between protein and nucleic acid, or even its most fundamental features, might have arisen in protocell droplets. All of today's DNA, strung through all the cells of apples and snakes, butterflies and buffaloes, is so universal that we have hardly any clues as to what the original machinery in those first self-perpetuating bodies might have looked like. Our most valuable insights seem to be provided by viruses and rings and grains of DNA (and occasionally by mysterious clumps of pure RNA) that invade cells and influence their metabolism. Minor chromosomes in bacteria (small ring-shaped molecules of DNA called plasmids), might be "naked genes" that entered the cells and took up permanent residence there aeons ago. They are by themselves capable of attacking and dismembering hydrocarbons, thus providing food for the bacterium; and they replicate and move off in opposite directions when the bacterium divides.

Researchers at General Electric have learned that each of the four different species of a bacterium belonging to the genus *Pseudomonas* possesses a different type of plasmid, each plasmid directing the production of a set of proteins capable of dismantling a different hydrocarbon component of crude oil. With the cleaning up of oil spills in mind, the General Electric team artificially transferred all four plasmid types into one bacterium. The newly introduced plasmids survided, and when the bacterium divided they followed the example and "superbug," a cell capable of metabolising two thirds of all known hydrocarbons, releasing carbon dioxide and water as waste products, was born. Amid fears of a possible *Cat's Cradle* scenario if "superbug" ever managed to establish a beachhead in an oil field, it was decided that the bacterium should not be used commercially. However, "superbug" does, by analogy, allow us to see how a primitive genetic apparatus might have found protection inside a protein droplet and immediately struck a symbiotic bond. This probably happened many times in many places, and all the startling special effects that life has produced are simply extensions and elaborations of those first genetic protocells. Interestingly, the engine of growth and reproduction, the DNA molecule, appears to have remained essentially unchanged.

Question: How likely was its emergence?

It could not have been impossible. It could not even have been very unlikely, because it is here. And it has been here for at least 3.5 billion years.

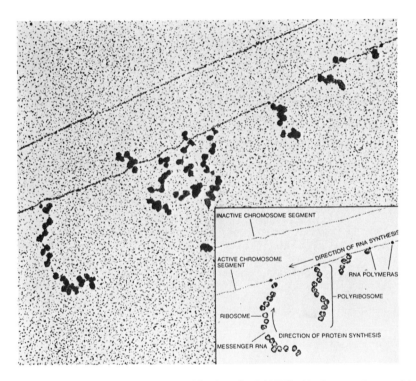

Bacterial DNA in action is shown at a magnification of 150,000X in this electron micrograph by O. L. Miller, Jr. An abbreviated interpretation of the micrograph (inset) shows two segments of an *Escherichia coli* chromosome. RNA polymerase molecules have attached themselves to the lower strand and have begun to catalyze the transcription of DNA into *messenger* RNA; one, at the far right, is at the approximate initiation site. Ribosomes have attached themselves to the growing *messenger* RNA strands, moving along them toward the chromosome, and translating the *messenger* RNA into protein (not shown). Inset *Courtesy of Scientific American. Micrograph reprinted from O. L. Miller, Jr., Barbara A. Hamkalo, and C. A. Thomas, Jr., Science, Vol. 169, pp. 392–395, 1970. Copyright 1970 by the American Association for the Advancement of Science.*

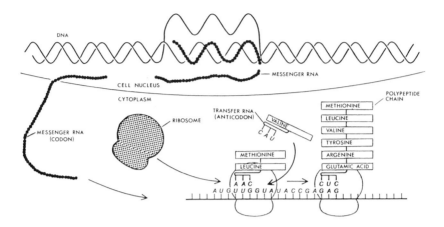

The major steps of protein synthesis, transcription and translation, occur respectively in the nucleus and cytoplasm of eucaryotic cells. The flow of information from DNA to *messenger* RNA to protein begins with the transcription of *messenger* RNA from relatively short segments of the DNA molecule. Information is stored in the DNA molecule as a linear code made up of four types of nucleotide base: adenine (A), cytosine (C), guanine (G), and thymine (T). Complimentary strands of RNA bear the same nucleotide bases as DNA (except for thymine, which is replaced by the closely related uracil, or U). This direct one-to-one copy of the DNA molecule contains "gibberish" sequences called introns (not shown); but before the RNA enters the cytoplasm, the introns are edited out by enzymes, and the strands of RNA that code for protein are spliced together by other enzymes to yield a short and "sensible" *messenger* RNA (exactly how and why this happens is, at this moment, a debatable subject). Expelled from the nucleus, the *messenger* RNA comes into contact with molecules of *ribosomal* and *transfer* RNA (both molecules are assembled and complexed with protein in the nucleus). The ribosomes then translate the *messenger* RNA into protein by means of complimentary *transfer* RNA molecules, which add amino acids one by one to growing chains as the ribosomes move along the *messenger* RNA strand. Each of the twenty amino acids found in protein molecules is specified by a "codon" made up of three sequential nucleotide bases on the *messenger* RNA.

In 1871 the English physicist John Tyndall wrote:

Darwin placed at the root of life a primordial germ, from which he conceived that the amazing richness and variety of life now upon the Earth's surface might have been deduced. If this hypothesis were true, it would not be final. The human imagination would infallibly look beyond the germ and, however hopeless the attempt, would inquire into the history of its genesis.

He could not have been more correct. We inquire, but at the present time we can only guess. Evidence for the evolution of genetic entities is so sparse that even flying saucers force themselves upon us. (Ah, but has anyone bothered to ask about the genesis of their pilots?)

One of the more plausible suggestions was made some 30 years ago by Norman H. Horowitz of the California Institute of Technology, and was more recently supported by Richard E. Dickerson of that same institution. They propose that a genetic coding system evolved, in a manner of speaking, "from back to front." Suppose, for example, that enzyme C is formed by the linking together of substance A and substance B (substances A and B representing simple associations of five or six amino acids), and that the sum of A and B is able to catalyze the polymerization of sugar phosphates into starch. The oldest need would then be for the polymerization of sugar phosphates and thus for enzyme C, and the oldest reaction would be the one that would make enzyme C from substances A and B. Assuming that substances A and B were raw materials obtained from the surroundings and that several million protocells in a given neighborhood were "consuming" substances A and B at rates exceeding their rate of production in the environment, a need might have arisen for the ability to make substances A and B from other, simpler raw materials; and some protocells might have successfully met this challenge, so that a series of metabolic steps would have began to evolve in reverse order.

What are the mechanism for making C from A and B; or A and B from simple amino acids?

University of Hawaii microbiologist Clair E. Folsome has visualized stable, circular molecules—small prototype generator RNAs—which acted both as templates for the production of very simple protein catalysts (say, four amino acids long) and as self-reproducing blueprints that could be carried inside protocells and distributed among their progeny. How might such a generator work? Let us consider a system consisting of a sugar-phosphate backbone (the basic skeleton of DNA and RNA molecules). Attached to each ribose sugar is one of the nucleic acid bases adenine (A), guanine (G), uracil (U), or cytosine (C). These bases are free to act as coding sequences for the production of RNA (ribonucleic acid) copies. According to base pairing rules, a passing guanine molecule, itself attached to a sugar and a phosphate (forming a nucleotide), will gravitate toward and form a weak hydrogen bond with an exposed cytosine on the circle. Similarly, uracil will attract adenine, adenine will attract uracil, and guanine will

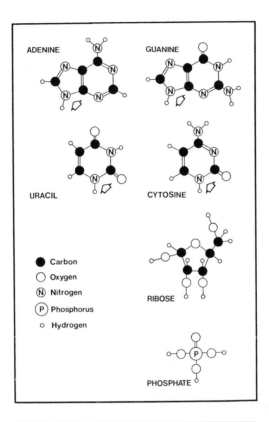

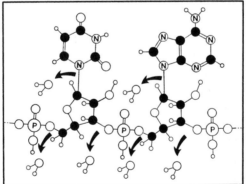

Molecules of ribonucleic acid (RNA) might have been the first carriers of genetic information. Each nucleotide of RNA consists of a ribose sugar bonded to a phosphate and one of four bases: adenine (A), guanine (G), uracil (U), or cytosine (C). The arrows indicate where the base joins to ribose in the formation of nucleotides.

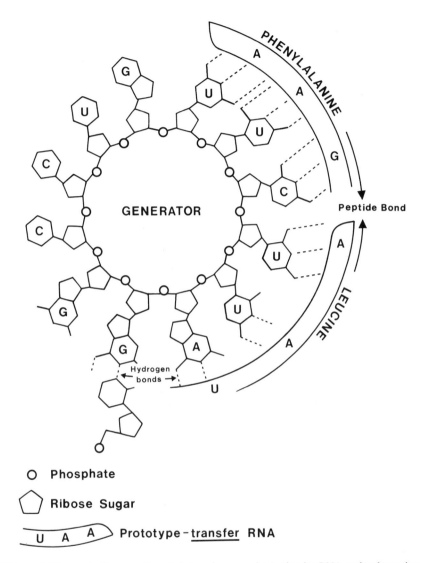

O Phosphate

⬠ Ribose Sugar

⬡ U A A⟩ Prototype – <u>transfer</u> RNA

This model for a primitive genetic code is based upon a short, circular RNA molecule serving both as a self-replicating carrier of information and as the template for protein synthesis. The *generator* RNA shown here is twelve nucleotides long and able to specify four amino acids. Prototype *transfer* RNAs, each carrying an attached amino acid, align themselves on the *generator* RNA according to base pairing rules (adenine bonds to uracil, cytosine to guanine). The amino acids can then form a simple protein by establishing peptide bonds (linking of the COOH group of one amino acid with the NH₂ group of another).

attract cytosine, until a second, outer circle—a copy complement of the generator RNA molecule—is formed.

If the outer circle were to be snipped open at some point and peeled slowly away from the generator RNA, nucleotides from the surroundings would begin to attach themselves to the freshly exposed nucleic acid bases, enabling the generator RNA and its copy complement to create replicas of each other. As in some presently living bacterial systems, the copying process might continue past the starting point to yield a longer replicate pair, leading to a generator sequence that repeats itself two or more times and to the production of longer protein molecules with multiple active sites. (The difficult part is getting the circular complements and corresponding amino acid sequences to peel away from each other.)

Strands composed of several nucleotides (polynucleotides) can twist, bend, and fold back on themselves. Rather than form a circlet of nucleotides, an RNA molecule may achieve stability by establishing hydrogen bonds between guanine and cytosine, uracil and adenine—back-bonding with itself—to produce a molecule with an open phosphate and hydroxyl group at one end and a protruding lobe of exposed nucleic acid bases at the other end: an analogue of the transfer RNA molecule.

University of Maryland molecular biologist Cyril Ponnamperuma has demonstrated that nucleotide sequences interact abiotically with amino acids in very precise ways. Though these interactions are not yet well understood, there has been speculation that projecting nucleic acid bases at one end of a primitive transfer RNA may create a ripple effect that resounds through the molecule and influences the behavior of exposed terminals at the opposite end. For example, a cytosine-cytosine-cytosine (CCC) triplet, located distally on an RNA lobe, could conceivably restrict the molecule's coupling activity to glycine or a closely related amino acid. In this way, back-bonded RNAs would come to be associated with specific amino acid types.

Now imagine a circular generator RNA molecule only twelve nucleotides long. Drifting through the interior of a protocell, or even riding naked in a warm shallow sea, the complex is a natural attractant for free-floating nucleic acid bases and will eventually acquire an outer ring of four primitive transfer RNAs, each carrying an attached amino acid. (Sometimes a nucleotide will arrive ahead of the transfer

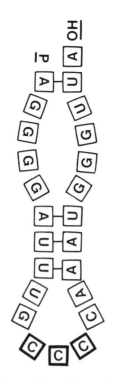

This prototype *transfer* RNA model, consisting of twenty-four nucleotides, was generated randomly by throwing a die with four of the faces representing adenine (A), guanine (G), uracil (U), and cytosine (C) until a linear molecule was constructed. When back-bonded with itself in a variety of ways, lobate protrusions reminiscent of the anticodon sites on modern *transfer* RNA molecules almost always result.

RNA, attaching itself to the circle and possibly blocking the transfer RNA's entry. The reverse can also occur, so that the processes of amino acid transfer and generator replication become slowed, if not confused. How nature overcame this and similar obstructions is not yet apparent.)

The amino acids, once introduced, can form a simple protein by establishing peptide bonds (linking of the carboxyl group of one amino acid with the amino group of another). We are no longer assembling amino acids randomly to make proteins. Each triplet of nucleotides (trinucleotide) on the generator RNA will attract or code for only one complement among the transfer RNAs. Thus a uracil-uracil-cytosine (UUC) base sequence will attract an adenine-adenine-guanine (AAG) complement of itself, which is likely to be the lobate end of a phenylalanine-carrying transfer RNA. The "instructions" to discriminate against all but those transfer RNAs most likely to be carrying phenylalanine could very well have been implanted by the transfer RNA molecule itself. Some generator RNAs may in fact have been constructed in reverse order from base sequences on the exposed lobes of back-bonded RNAs. Once produced, the generators would function much like photographic negatives, upon which the appropriate transfer RNAs, linked with amino acids, could gather. (The generator RNAs might also produce copy complements that back-bond to become short transfer RNAs.)

At this point an important problem arises. The three exposed bases of present-day transfer RNA molecules are matched to the correct bases on the *messenger* RNA by highly evolved ribosomal proteins. How can a system like the one described here match the right transfer RNAs (which, of course, means the right amino acids) to the right nucleotide triplets without these structures? Possibly it can not. In our hypothetical ring of four triplets, in the absence of ribosomes, the first transfer RNA to arrive on the scene can attach itself at any appropriate point on the circle. A UUCUU sequence on the generator RNA will attract a transfer RNA with a projecting AAG sequence to the UUC site (we will assume that this molecule is carrying phenylalanine). But a molecule of serine-bearing transfer RNA with an exposed AGA may arrive there first and bind to the UCU site, or a leucine-bearing molecule to the CUU site, so that three different proteins can be derived from the same generator sequence. However, random starting sites are not necessarily a threat to the continued survival of amino acid rings. Most amino acids fall into one of four distinct groups: the basic, such as argenine, which contain more amine groups (NH$^+$) than carboxyl groups (COOH$^-$); the acidic, such as aspartic acid, which contain more carboxyl groups than amine groups; the aliphatic, such as leucine and phenylalanine, consisting only of a carbon skeleton and one each of carboxyl and amine groups; and the polar, such as serine, with hydroxyl groups (OH) added. A small, four-amino-acid-long protein molecule possessing useful catalytic abilities might function with any of a variety of amino acids of *the same class* at a particular place on the molecule without any significant loss of potency. Argenine and lysine, for example, are both basic

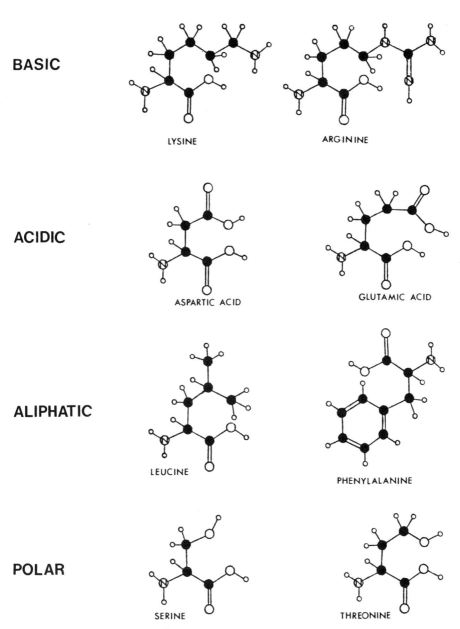

BASIC

LYSINE

ARGININE

ACIDIC

ASPARTIC ACID

GLUTAMIC ACID

ALIPHATIC

LEUCINE

PHENYLALANINE

POLAR

SERINE

THREONINE

Most amino acids fall into one of four distinct classes: the basic (amino acids with more NH$^+$ groups than COOH$^-$ groups), the acidic (with more COOH$^-$ groups than NH$^+$ groups), the aliphatic (with one each of COOH$^-$ and NH$^+$ groups), and the polar (with OH groups added). Members of each class possess similar properties. Therefore, early genes need only have specified, one at a time, any of four classes of amino acids rather than twenty-odd different amino acids.

amino acids possessing highly reactive nitrogen groups, and one could easily be substituted for the other. Returning to our four-trinucleotide ring, if a leucine-bearing transfer RNA molecule arrives ahead of a phenylalanine-bearing transfer RNA and, failing to encounter any repulsive forces in the UUCUU region, becomes associated by weak hydrogen bonds with the CUU site, the substitution should not make the resulting protein incapable of acting. Leucine and phenylalanine are both aliphatic amino acids possessing similar properties; but substitution of either of these with serine, a polar amino acid, may inactivate the protein or entirely alter its function. The "trick," then, is to construct active protein catalysts from sequences consisting only of a handful of amino acids. The amino acids are drawn, one at a time, from one of four classes (rather than one of twenty-odd different amino acids).

Chemistry provides the raw material: random, unguided variation, constrained only by associative and repulsive forces, and the geometry of bonded atoms. Some generator sequences (and their RNA copy complements, which may become generator RNAs in their own right) are bound to code for totally functionless proteins. Others may produce a useful enzyme, but only when amino acids join to form one of three possible combinations, so that the efforts of protein production are wasted two out of three times. A protocell loaded down with either of these two generating systems may not have many generations of descendents in its future. Darwinian selection now enters the picture, fashioning the raw material of variation by preserving those systems that, under prevailing conditions of the day, work best (right-handed amino acids must have been bad at something that left-handed amino acids can do). In our model population of protocells equipped with generator RNAs, natural selection will foster those generator systems able to produce useful proteins at least two thirds of the time. The optimal arrangement is a set of nucleotides that will either code for the same sequence of amino acid classes regardless of where transfer RNAs start attaching themselves to the generator complement or, if it must produce two or three proteins with different properties, will give rise to two or three viable proteins.

Early protocells probably had very slow metabolisms, doubling their mass and dividing perhaps once every 200 years or so. Generator and transfer RNAs able to produce active proteins, and able to produce them in the shortest span of years (or months), would have been at a premium. Protocells containing these RNAs (or something very much like them) would, on average, produce more successful off-spring. Moreover, a tendency for protocells to clump together and then separate under strong currents (as demonstrated by Fox) could lead to the exchange of RNA between different protocells. (The invention of sex, by protocells, would thus have preceded the appearance of true chromosomes.) Finally, and most significantly, this exchange can result in the transfer from one protocell to another protocell of generator molecules that enable both to survive, even though they may be competing for resources in the same environment. In other words, the prototype genetic coding systems possessed the ability to promote their own survival regardless of the fate of their host protocells. Add to this the potential to generate longer copy complements with multiple active sites and the capacity to do so with occasional er-

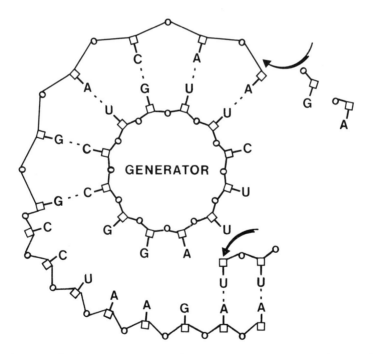

Replication of a circular *generator* RNA molecule to produce a long repetition of a single ancestral gene.

rors (which natural selection may destroy or preserve), and the surface of the infant Earth becomes awash with infinite possibilities.*

The nuclei of present-day cells direct molecules to recognize other molecules and to hold onto each other or let go of each other in extraordinarily precise ways, producing structures as diverse as eyelashes, retinal cones, and maple leaves. The ropes of DNA contained in one of the trees from which this book is made, if lined end to end, would reach to the sun and back over 300 times; yet they occupy a total volume no bigger than an ice cube. We have come a long way on a little skeleton of sugars and phosphates studded with nucleic acid bases.

---

*A more recent example of gene duplication has been proposed by California Institute of Technology geneticist Edward B. Lewis. Eight genes, all situated in sequence side-by-side, regulate the development of the larval fruit fly's posterior body segments into the specialized divisions of the adult abdomen. Lewis argues that these eight regulator genes arose as repititions of a single ancestral gene and that they then evolved in different directions.

7
All This and Heaven Too?

Crystals display a high degree of organization, but orderliness is not enough. If it were, then the conversion of Lot's wife into a pillar of salt should be regarded as the most dramatic evolutionary advance of all time.

A.G. Cairns-Smith

We saw things as falling apart, degenerating, entropy taking over. Things de-evolving into their similar, simplistic state.

Mark Mothersbaugh

There is a simplicity in the whole scheme, so much so that you almost feel the whole universe is trying to make life. With the knowledge of organic chemistry from the work we've done, I'm willing to say that eventually we'll define life as a property of the carbon atom. The first thing I tell my students is that a professor in the constellation Andromeda is teaching the same course I am.

Cyril Ponnamperuma

Pouring off from every young star is an unquenchable tumult of raw energy. Most of that energy is lost—wasted—destined never to strike matter anywhere in the vast, unfillable sink of outer space. But there are obstructions: a pebble here . . . a hydrogen atom there . . . a planet . . . an atmosphere. And where energy does splash up against matter, it must invariably cause changes in it.

Within several thousand kilometers of our sun the sheer pressure of the energetic photons of light is strong enough to propel you away. Even at a distance of 60 million kilometers (approximately 37 million miles), the surface of Mercury is powdery, pounded, and dry, its sky dominated by a broad yellow-white globe. Airless—dead as the lunar maria—the planet is baked by an unrelenting shower of heat and light. Gases, if they were present at all, would blaze instantly and stream away into space. The heaviest as well as the lightest of metals would quickly soften, bubble, and boil. Here the elements seem condemned to disorder by the celestial din of a nearby star.

Farther away—much farther—the radiant energy has dissipated, spread out over so much emptiness. The surfaces of wandering, stony objects are lit only faintly in this place where the roiling sun is little more than a distant bright star. The steady trickle of energy is too feeble to animate the elements. Carbon dioxide, methane, and water (things once vaporous) have condensed out here, solidified and accumulated—crystalline, unchanging.

Somewhere between these two regions is a boundary area where matter is neither fried nor frozen, but heated at just the right temperature. Such a regime is found around every singular star (and members of binaries if, like Alpha Centauri A and B, their habitable zones do not touch or overlap), although the boundaries may advance and retreat as the stellar energy output fluctuates. If a planet is set aloft within this zone, and if it possesses sufficient mass to support the right kind of atmosphere, then sooner or later carbon, hydrogen, oxygen, nitrogen, phosphorus, and sulfur will emerge from their prolonged exile in disorder and will bind themselves together, forming structures of ever increasing complexity.

The rest is clear going. Impelled by a steady flow of radiant energy, the once inanimate elements are transformed into a symphony of molecular architecture, always moving, always changing, segregating in solution, and evolving cycles for the storage and release of energy and, finally, a primitive metabolism.

Very few people will deny that life can evolve on a planet like Earth. But the possibility of its occurrence elsewhere, outside Earth, has tugged at man's imagination for immemorial years. Only recently has our species developed the ability to leap off the Earth and steal fleeting glimpses of other worlds. We are children with strange new senses—probing, touching, tasting, turning over rocks and poking our fingers underneath.

On the moon and inner planets we have found dust in great abun-

Early afternoon on the Plain of Chryse, as seen from *Viking Lander 1* on August 4, 1976. The landscape is reminiscent of some desert regions on Earth; however, the sands of Mars are apparently lacking even the simplest organic molecules. Dust there is, but no allergens. *Provided through the courtesy of National Aeronautics and Space Administration, California Institute of Technology, Jet Propulsion Laboratories.*

dance, but no allergens. The *Viking Missions* revealed Mars as a planet probably untouched by life. The organic content of its soil, over a broad range of molecules from one- or two-carbon compounds (like methane and ethane) to napthalene (better known as "moth balls"), is generally below some parts per billion.

Directly the *Viking Landers* arrived and ingested the dust and air. Organic molecules, supplied by the experiments from Earth, were immediately assailed and dismembered by corrosive superoxides ($Fe_2 O_3$) in the soil. It is now apparent that powerful oxidizing agents, formed by ultraviolet decomposition of the carbon dioxide atmosphere, have rendered the Martian wilderness sterile and lifeless.

Ironically, the quest for Earth-like biochemistry may soon focus not on Mars but on its tiny inner satellite, Phobos. According to measurements made by the *Viking Orbiter-1* spacecraft, Phobos

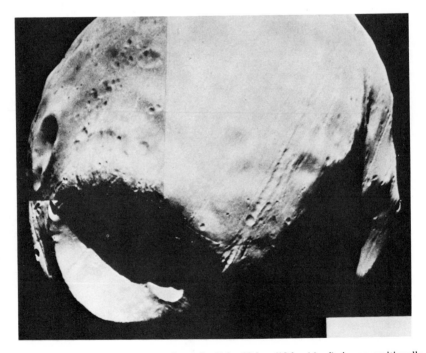

Mars' inner satellite Phobos, measuring only 19 by 22 km (12 by 14 mi), is compositionally similar to the carbonaceous chondrite meteorites, which have been found to contain organic molecules of striking complexity. *Provided through the courtesy of National Aeronautics and Space Administration, California Institute of Technology, Jet Propulsion Laboratories.*

(whose spectral signature coincides almost exactly with the asteroids Ceres and Pallas) is similar in composition to Type I carbonaceous chondrite meteorites. An appreciable number of these meteorites contain as much as six to eight percent carbon (the most abundant element in this part of the universe after hydrogen, helium, and oxygen). As we have seen in chapter 5, the carbon matrix of the Type I carbonaceous chondrites is literally laced with organic molecules, including fatty acids, amino acids, alcohols, sugars, purines, and pyrimidines.

Perhaps the most striking examples of molecular ornamentation thus far identified in meteorites are porphyrins, first discovered in samples of the Orgueil meteorite by two Canadian biochemists, Hodgson and Baker, in 1964. The porphyrins (or closely related compounds) are common to almost all terrestrial organisms. The inclusion of iron or other metals in their centers allows them to function ideally as electron transfer catalysts. In animals they have become the foundations for oxygen-carrying blood pigments. The magnesium porphyrin, because of its tendency to act as an "electron racetrack" when struck by energy from the sun, was incorporated into living cells as an

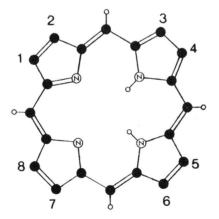

The skeleton of a porphyrin molecule, consisting basically of four pyrrole rings linked together by four methane bridges to form a flattened cyclic molecule. Specific porphyrins differ in having various organic groups attached onto positions 1 through 8, and in complexing with a metallic ion (such as Mg, Cu, or Fe) at the center of the molecule. Porphyrins are common to almost all terrestrial organisms, and have also been found in some carbonaceous meteorites.

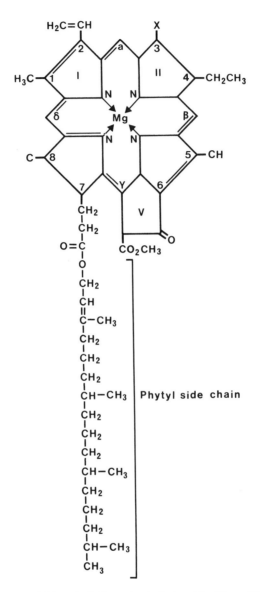

The structure of chlorophyll, the molecule that sustains life on this planet.

energy storage molecule. Retained, it ultimately evolved into chlorophyll, the molecule that sustains life on this planet.

Organic pigments extracted from the Orgueil meteorite appear distinct from those found on Earth, ruling out the possibility of earthly contamination. Chlorins, a group of compounds closely related to the porphyrins, are plant-related pigments that differ from porphyrins in that they have two "extra" hydrogen atoms added to the basic porphyrin structure. Terrestrial dusts, soils, and recent sediments—the possible contaminants—contain a wealth of chlorins far outnumbering the porphyrins. In carbonaceous chondrites, however, the exact opposite appears to be true; the chlorins are virtually absent. This finding makes sense only if the Orgueil porphyrins are indigenous to the meteorite, and such anomalies are expected if the origin of these compounds lies in some preliving chemical process rather than in the tissues of terrestrial plants and animals.

Several researchers have found evidence that suggests the parent body or bodies that gave rise to carbonaceous chondrites provided a warm, moist environment with an alkaline pH and slightly reducing conditions: ideal conditions for producing organic molecules. But where could such bodies have existed?

Radiometric methods of dating have placed the formation of carbonaceous chondrites roughly 4.6 billion years ago, a time when the primordial cloud of gas and dust was rapidly evolving into the sun, planets, meteorites, and other debris of the solar system. The ingredients of the primordial nebula almost certainly accumulated from the ejecta of exploded stars, ultimately finding their way into such things as the pages on which these words are printed, the glue and fabric that binds them, and your hand that holds them.

Recent data suggest that interstellar grains of unusual isotopic composition, synthesized by the lives and deaths of stars, were stirred into the rock material of the carbonaceous chondrites even as they accreted to form the parent bodies. For example, the Murchison meteorite has yielded an unusual xenon component, believed to have been forged in the interior of a giant red sun. Nuggets of material extracted from the Allende meteorite exhibit peculiar isotopic ratios that imply the occurrence of a nearby supernova just prior to the onset of condensation and fractionation events within the presolar nebula. Consequently, the organic molecules of carbonaceous meteorites seem to exist side-by-side with the outgassed fusion products of stars.

How did amino acids, sugars, porphyrins, and other advanced products of organic chemistry come to be associated with the wreckage of stars? If we suppose that the Orgueil porphyrins originated on some primordial planet that has since broken up, then we are also forced to accept a series of very unlikely events whose probability goes down with their multiplication. We must, for example, consider how nuggets of preplanetary matter (aluminum 26, for instance) might survive planet formation and the tremendous geological pressures and heating that would follow. Furthermore, a planet with gravity sufficient to hold an atmosphere and water on its surface does not simply break itself apart and go scattering its pieces about the solar system.

If, instead, we imagine the Orgueil, Murchison, and Allende meteorites as splinters of minor planets that were too small to possess atmospheres—much less pools, tidal flats, and rivers—and if we suppose that they came from places more distant (and less hospitable) than Mars, then how were those first steps in the direction of life taken?

To answer this question we must first try to visualize the origin of the carbonaceous chondrites. The presolar nebula apparently contained the cold, carbon-rich ejecta of at least a handful of dead stars. Initially, any residual carbon compounds—hydrogen cyanide, formaldehyde, cyanoacetylene, and Carl Sagan's rings—must have existed as frozen, inanimate molecules. However, the collapse, aggregation, and packing together of cosmic dust dramatically altered that condition. Even small accumulations of rock, perhaps approximating Phobos in size, would have been heated by relatively short-lived radioactive elements. At the centers of these bodies, temperatures possibly climbed as high as 2,000°C (3,632°F), as would seem to be indicated by the presence of partially remelted silicates in some carbonaceous chondrites. The mean surface temperature, on the other hand, would have remained generally below 0°C. Somewhere between the cold, airless surface and the molten or nearly molten core there existed a zone of thickness measured in kilometers where temperatures ranged betwen the freezing and boiling points of water. (Such zones are referred to by the authors as Fox Holes, named after University of Miami molecular biologist Sidney Fox, for his work with the thermal synthesis of very large molecules from simple organic compounds.)

Could this be the source of the warm, stable environment proposed by some planetary scientists? The original heating up of the parent bodies made the emergence of such zones inevitable, and, assuming that the right kinds of atoms were present, they certainly look like potential sites for the synthesis of organic compounds.

A hollow space in the Allende meteorite, some 3.4 mm across, was partly filled in by pyrrhotite crystals, a form of iron sulfide, which grew from the outer margin inward (presumably with falling temperature). The crystals imply an episode of secondary mineralization inside the meteorite parent body. This inclusion cannot be explained by the condensation of solids from a gas in the solar nebula (as some planetary geologists suggest), as no model can adequately describe how this may lead to the formation of a hollow space partly filled in by later condensates. Such evidence is in support of the hypothesis that many of the organic compounds found in meteorites—perhaps most—post-date formation of the solar system and were produced by secondary processes inside planetesimals. The rectangle in the center of the photograph indicates the area covered at the top of page 92. *Photo by C. R. Pellegrino and M. Loper.*

Let's look a little closer at this idea. Some of the basic constituents of carbonaceous chondrites would have furnished criteria for a hypothetical environment inside the warm, intermediate layers of a parent body. There was water: this is shown not only by the presence of indigenous water, but also by mineralized structures such as magnetite spherules (Fe_3O_4), microgeodes, and veins of magnesium sulfate ($MgSO_4$), whose formation appears to have required the presence of liquid water. The matrix, or groundmass, of carbonaceous chondrites, consists largely of very fine particles of silicate minerals, some occurring as stacked micaceous sheets. The total sur-

High-resolution pictures of pyrrhotite crystals (Fe_7S_8) covering the walls of a spheroidal cavity in the Allende meteorite. Rectangular markings indicate the areas covered by the two pictures on the bottom. The crystals, bronze-yellow in color, display the characteristic hexagonal morphology of pyrrhotite grains. Other morphologies represent broken or partly obscured crystals. As its chemical formula suggests, pyrrhotite formation requires a high ratio of sulfur to iron, which is difficult to achieve in a nebula of solar composition, again pointing to an origin via secondary mineralization inside a planetismal. *Photos by C. R. Pellegrino and M. Loper.*

This field of pyrrhotite crystals (*top*) was discovered in a hollow space between two layers in the Murchison meteorite. *Photo by C. R. Pellegrino.* Note the resemblance to the cluster of pyrrhotite platelets (*bottom*) recovered in hot (380° ± 30°C) water emanating from hydrothermal vents 2.6 kilometers (1.6 miles) under the east Pacific Ocean. *Photo courtesy of J. D. Mac-*

dougall and Scripps Institution. From Science, vol. 207, pp. 1421–1433, 1980. Copyright 1980 by the American Association for the Advancement of Science. Although the morphology of the Murchison crystals is consistent with formation in the presence of hot water, pyrrhotite is also known from volcanic rocks that have never seen aqueous mineralization (scale bars = 10μ).

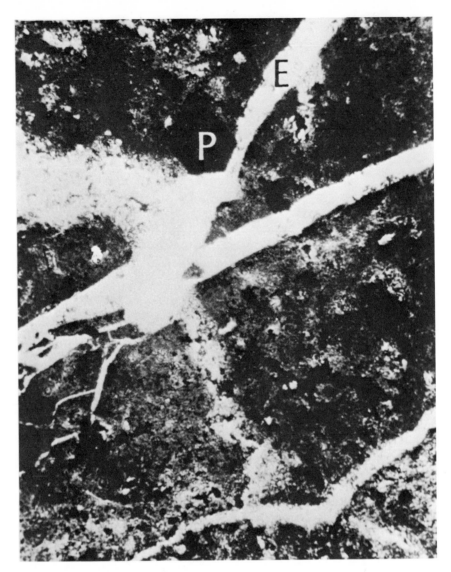

The hexagonal pyrrhotite crystal (P) Fe_7S_8, shown in this thin section of the Orgueil meteorite protrudes into a vein of epsomite (E), $Mg\ SO_4.7H_2O$, a form of magnesium sulfate. Although the formula for epsomite is itself suggestive of deposition by liquid water, supporters of the "dry asteroid model" have argued that the epsomite might have been formed by a gas containing sulfur dioxide and oxygen. However, the association of pyrrhotite with the epsomite shows clearly that this could not be the case because a gas containing oxidized sulfur would have dissolved the pyrrhotite crystal. The intact pyrrhotite requires that the magnesium sulfate be transported into the cracks by liquid water. *Courtesy of J. F. Kerridge and the Institute of Geophysics, University of California.*

face area accessible to water and organic compounds percolating through the grains was therefore enormous, providing excellent substrates for the capture and concentration of prebiological molecules. Furthermore, the abundance of negative and positive charges carried by the silicates and associated metals could have served to bind charged molecules to the grains, and also might have enabled them to act as primitive catalytic centers. In short, the insides of the parent bodies were wet and suitable for chemical activity.

But this was to pass.

The decay of radioactive elements could sustain the warmth for only a short time, perhaps a half billion years or so—a mere fortnight in terms of the solar system. One can easily imagine the intermediate prebiological zone sinking deeper and deeper into the interior of a planetesimal, until finally the glow went out and its depths became frozen. Meanwhile, the planets formed.

How far could chemical evolution have gone? Could life have formed inside the minor planets? Having established on several grounds that the organic compounds contained in carbonaceous meteorites originated outside of the Earth, what remains to be settled is whether they are preliving organic matter or the actual products of cellular life. Although the evidence weighs heavily in favor of the preliving hypothesis, the presence of ambiguous microfossils (or pseudofossils) in carbonaceous chondrites does raise questions as to how far molecular evolution might have advanced in the meteorite parent bodies.

The microstructures, cautiously named "organized elements," range from 5 to 30 microns in diameter and fall generally into two classes. Particles of the first class are more numerous and are probably native to the meteorites. But they are rather featureless objects and seem to lack specific properties indicative of once-living microfossils. The class 2 particles are quite rare. They exhibit highly structured forms, clearly biogenic, but the majority of them show a strong resemblance to pollen grains and other common airborne contaminants. Indeed, some of the spiny class 2 elements have been identified as ragweed pollen by several pollen experts, and one carbonaceous chondrite belonging to the authors yielded a diatom shell that could be traced to a species living in Lake Victoria, Africa.

In 1963, Dr. Bartholomew Nagy of the University of Arizona and

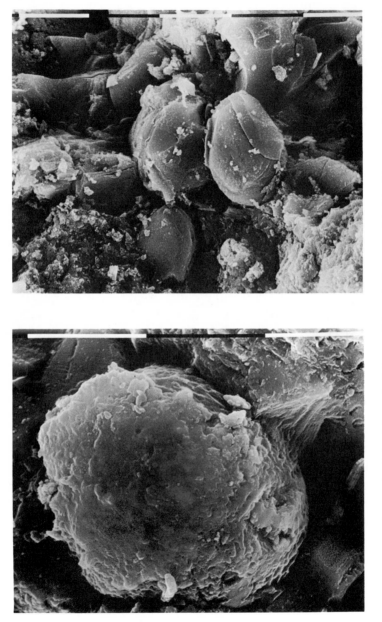

Scanning electron micrographs of class 1 "organized elements" shown in the matrix of the Murchison meteorite. The scale bars (*right*) indicate 10 μ. *Photos by C. R. Pellegrino and K. Goldie.*

96

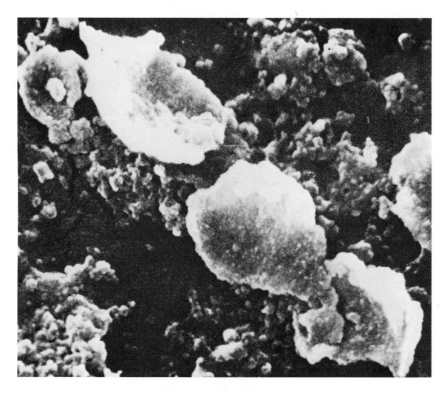

Scanning electron micrograph of a hollow sphere from the Orgueil meteorite, broken to show the thickness and elasticity of the wall. The cup-shaped fragments are approximately 5 μ in diameter. Removal and "dissection" of class one "organized elements" yields evidence suggesting that most are organic shells absorbed onto the surface of mineral spheroids. *M. Rossignol-Strick, E. S. Bargmoorn—Extraterrestrial abiogenic organizations of organic matter: the hollow spheres of the Orgueil meteorite. Space Life Science, 3 (1971) 89–107.*

his co-workers sought to determine whether "organized elements" might simply be false alarms, triggered perhaps by artifacts or "jokes of nature," such as mineral spheroids or hexagons that mimic or give the appearance of being microfossils. From several meteorites they extracted small, rounded, class 1 objects, and investigated them with an electron microprobe. They found some to be laden with silicates or limonite (hydrated ferric oxide). When the mineral constituents were removed with the aid of acids, the majority of these microstructures dissolved completely out of existence, which supported the proposition that they were natural mineral formations. Nevertheless, a few

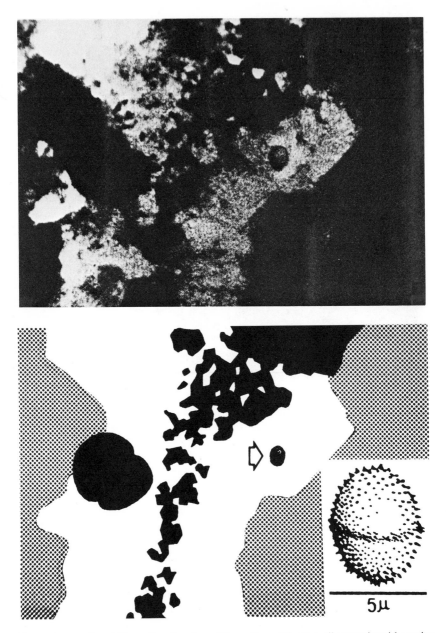

Photomicrograph and illustration showing a thin section of the Orgueil meteorite with a spiny class two "organized element" embedded in a salt vein. *Illustration redrawn; original illustration and photo courtesy of B. Nagy.*

left residues or bodies that could be seen under a microscope: round, acid-insoluble "shells" that contained no elements heavier than magnesium, indicating that the objects were possibly composed of carbon-based material.

It is thus tempting to suggest that these structures are a residue of life in meteorites that became impregnated with minerals, "fossilized" in much the same way as terrestrial microfossils are formed. They closely resemble the oldest protocell-like objects known on Earth (approximately 3.76 billion years old, excavated from the Isua micaceous mataquartzite deposits of Greenland) and are identical to organic microstructures produced on water surfaces during spark-discharge experiments.

In still another experiment, spheroidal microstructures separated from the Mokoia meteorite (which fell in New Zealand in 1908) were shown to take up various biological stains. During control experiments in which meteorite fragments were heated overnight at 700°C and the stain test repeated, absorption did not occur. This

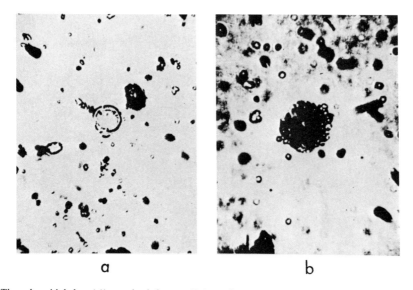

a   b

The spheroidal class 1 "organized elements" shown here were recovered from crushed preparations of the Mokoia meteorite. Such formations bear a striking resemblance to the products of spark-discharge experiments. Magnification (*a*) 400X, (*b*) 630X. *Provided through the courtesy of National Aeronautics and Space Administration, California Institute of Technology, Jet Propulsion Laboratory.*

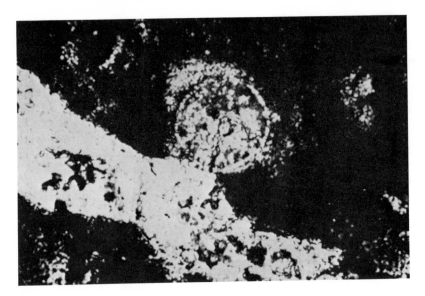

Petrographic thin section of the Orgueil meteorite, showing a spheroidal class 1 "organized element" embedded in the mineral matrix. *Copyright 1966 by the American Association for the Advancement of Science. Courtesy of H. C. Urey.*

Acid-insoluble residues of class one "organized elements" from the Mighei meteorite, which fell in Ukraine in 1899, are magnified 600X. *Copyright 1966 by the American Association for the Advancement of Science. Courtesy of H. C. Urey.*

result would be expected if the meteorite contained organic particles, since they would be destroyed by the high temperature.

Although this might appear to have a bearing on the interpretation of lifelike signatures in meteorites, two important points must be evaluated: First, spheroids are a very common equilibrium form in nature (their universality is displayed in the shapes of objects as diverse as stars, planets, protein droplets, pollen grains, and soap bubbles), and, second, the results described here would be reproduced exactly if the class 1 "organized elements" were in fact nothing more glamorous than organic compounds adsorbed onto mineral grains.

Currently, researchers are of the general opinion that some of the Mokoia microstructures are mineral grains, while others are associations of sulfur droplets and hydrocarbons, presumably of noncellular origin.

In view of recent theories of chemical evolution, it would be most surprising not to find complex organic particles or protocells existing coincidentally with amino acids, porphyrins, and other carbon compounds in carbonaceous meteorites. As we have seen in the previous chapter, small organic molecules (such as amino acids) are synthesized easily in the laboratory by subjecting mixtures of primeval gases (typically methane and ammonia) to electrical discharges over water. Invariably, highly polymeric material is also produced, appearing during the first 24 hours as an accumulation of dark matter on the walls of the reaction vessel and as a thin oily film on the water's surface. If the water is agitated or made to splash against the walls of the flask, the polymers separate from the surface to form organic microstructures ranging in size from 1 to 40 microns. Usually they are spheroidal bodies with textured surfaces and clearly structured interiors, but molecular biologists have described a remarkable variety of form and structure, including delicate tube-shaped objects with hollow interiors and occasional hints of septa.*

---

* Apparently, spheroids and long hollow tubes with partitions (or the beginnings of partitions), manifested as evenly spaced thickenings of the tube wall, are equilibrium forms naturally assumed by polymers. Their behavior does not seem unlike that of fresh-blown soap bubbles, which form spontaneously into such familiar, stable shapes as hollow globes and hemispherical doublets. Organic microstructures obey the same laws and must also seek stability. The products of spark-discharge experiments may thus have a bearing on one of Stephen Jay Gould's great puzzlements: the origin of multicellularity in plants and animals. Multicellularity might have

Virtually the entire gamut of "organized elements" observed in meteorites and terrestrial Precambrian rocks is represented in the products of spark-discharge experiments. Similar particles were probably present in our own seas, and also in the warm layers of the meteorite parent bodies, from the very moment that simple organic molecules came into being.

Clair Folsome and Andrew Brittain at the University of Hawaii have studied model protocells produced by electrical discharges and found them to possess low-level metabolic abilities. For example, if the model protocells are provided with water, a nitrogen-hydrogen atmosphere, and long-wavelength ultraviolet radiation as an energy source, they can synthesize formaldehyde and related organic compounds—including small quantities of amino acids—from carbonate ($CO_3^=$). With hollow interiors and with membranes acting as barriers against the outside world, each protocell carries within itself the potential for isolating chemical reactions and for evolving a primitive metabolism. They are not life, but they are getting close to it.

The consideration of protocell evolution leads logically to a need for defining exactly when highly ordered associations of common elements cross the line between chemical and biological evolution. Life is an elusive thing to define. To quote Clair Folsome, "it wiggles away whenever approached." Assemble any three biologists in one place—or worse yet a whole auditorium full of them—and ask them to solve this apparently simple problem: You might have a war on your hands. The arguments—accusations, even—will rage for days. Inevitably, somebody will drag rocks and salt crystals onto the podium and present them as candidates for life. Why not? They grow and break apart and reproduce themselves. And they outnumber us! They are probably the most successful things around. Shortly after this (we

---

arisen several times, therefore either or both of the two prevailing scenarios—amalgamation (individual cells came together and began to live as colonies) and division (colonies developed from partitions forming within individual cells)—may be correct. A third potential scenario, implied by spark-discharge microtubules (and also by clumping behavior demonstrated by Fox, Oparin, and Folsome microspheroids), calls for the existence of multichambered entities even before the emergence of anything that might qualify as truly living. In essence, then, physics decreed that the structural homologues (features similar by descent, for example, the forelimbs of people, birds, seals, and tigers) shared by spirogyra and a blade of grass were present from the very start—almost from the first moments of chemical evolution—among lifeless, randomly assembled organic molecules.

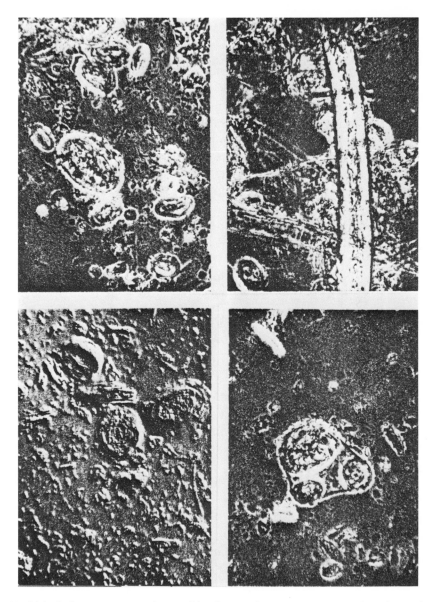

Nonbiological processes are quite capable of generating an enormous number of organic microstructures, as illustrated by these photomicrographs taken after twenty hours of electrical discharge through a mixture of methane and nitrogen over water. In a typical spark-discharge experiment, more than 60 percent of the total carbon present in the methane is recovered as organic microstructures like these. Generally, they are hollow and exhibit complex external and internal morphologies. The larger objects shown here are approximately 20 microns in diameter. *Courtesy of C. E. Folsome.*

guarantee it), someone will propose horters (or something like them) with DNA based on the silicon atom. But atoms of silicon simply do not work that way: No matter what temperature you cook them at, or how long you cook them, they do not form double or triple bonds to create, for example, a siliceous version of acetylene (Si $\equiv$ Si). Even if this were possible, a mixture of triple-bonded silicon molecules would probably resemble quartz, whereas acetylene (HC $\equiv$ CH) is a gas. In spite of nearly 4 billion years of chemical and biological evolution on this planet, and a world-wide abundance of silicon, the element appears nowhere as part of a functional enzyme, only as structural molecules like the glassy, venom-filled needles with which single-celled helizoids capture prey, or the honeycomb-like skeletons of certain rare and beautiful sponges. "Ahah! But there *is* silicon-based life!" someone will argue. "The chips in a *Viking Lander's* computer banks contain a volume of information equivalent to at least the number of genetic coding sequences strung through the DNA of a typical virus." To which a skeptical voice is bound to reply, "Where do you get off calling a virus life?" The meeting may proceed to name-calling and then deteriorate from that point.

For tens of centuries, men have scrutinized the forests and separated the trees from the mosses and insects and pack rats. The rocks, and the chemicals from which they are made, have been dissected and classified. We have divided all of nature—even ecology, its most unifying and indivisible property—into categories for human convenience. We humans display an overwhelming compulsion to classify things, yet, in spite of this (or perhaps because of it), when we try to determine which of those things are alive, we stumble headlong over ourselves.

Cyril Ponnamperuma, director of the Laboratory for Chemical Evolution at the University of Maryland, recommends a gradational approach to the definition of life:

> The division of matter into living and nonliving is perhaps an artificial one, convenient for distinguishing such extreme cases as a man and a stone but quite inappropriate when describing other cases such as a virus particle. Indeed, the crystallization of a virus by Wendell Stanley brought about the need for revising our definition of "life" and "living"... . Pirie has compared our use of liv-

ing and nonliving to the words acid and base as used in chemistry. While sodium hydroxide is distinctly alkaline, sulfuric acid is a powerful acid. But, in between these two extremes is a whole variation in strength. The chemist has overcome the confusion arising from these rigid categories by inventing the nomenclature of "hydrogen-ion concentration." In this way, all the observed phenomena can be described in terms of one quantity, pH. We may have to invent a similar quantity to avoid any vagueness that might arise in applying the term "life" to borderline cases such as the virus.

Thus, even self-reproducing protocells, Oparin's coacervates, for example, may find a niche at the lower end of a pH scale for life. Carbonaceous chondrites apparently contain the very foundations of the scale: precursor organic particles from which advanced life forms could have later evolved. If such an organization of matter can be duplicated in two or more places in the same solar system, then the union of carbon, hydrogen, oxygen, nitrogen, phosphorus, and sulfur is seemingly not an unusual occurrence. Consequently, as we continue to look outward from our Earth, we should not be surprised to find this part of the universe rippling with organic chemistry, and perhaps more. . . .

8
Ice

There is increasing recognition of a new science of extraterrestrial life; sometimes called exobiology—a curious development in view of the fact that this "science" has yet to demonstrate that its subject matter exists!

George G. Simpson

There is no question that there is an unseen world. The problem is, how far is it from midtown and how late is it open?

Woody Allen

Life from nonlife. You could start the process in your own kitchen, if you wanted to. It's that easy. Assemble carbon, hydrogen, nitrogen, and oxygen in one place (methane and ammonia gas over water will do nicely), apply heat, shock waves, X-rays, or ultraviolet radiation—almost any form of energy input—and, invariably, within twenty hours or so, you will have incited the formation of carbon compounds ranging from simple amino acids to complex organic microstructures resembling spheroids, rods, and hollow tubes with tantalizing septalike divisions. Yet such experiments involve only small volumes over very short periods of time. What could be done with entire oceans over a period of millions, or billions, of years? You need only look out your window or into a mirror to see.

For more than two decades, the human species has sought possible signatures of life elsewhere in the solar system. Indeed, fifty-three different amino acids, microscopic balls of organic matter, and flattened, ring-shaped porphyrin molecules similar to (but distinct from) chlorophyll have been found inside carbonaceous meteorites. Though their extraterrestrial origin is no longer in doubt, it appears unlikely that any of these substances will ever be identified with the machinery of once-living cells. Instead, they may ultimately be regarded as the very precursors from which bacteria or algae-like cells might have later evolved, given just the right temperature for about 500 million years or so. We might conclude, then, that the carbon atom will infallibly move in the direction of organic chemistry and, if the right conditions prevail long enough, toward life. But nowhere else in the vicinity of the sun have we seen it duplicated.

From our Earth we have sent ambassadors—magnesium spheres and insects with senses and voices and eyes of their own. We even went directly to the moon, putting human hands and feet into the matter. And one by one we have crossed the planets off as potential sites for the synthesis of life. Saturn's largest satellite, Titan, was the latest to fall. Probing its clouds with an infrared eye, *Voyager 1* found temperatures ranging near −203° C (−333° F) about 50 to 70 kilometers (31 to 44 miles) above the surface, and −181° C (−293° F) at ground level. At those temperatures the petals of a rose become as rigid and fragile as a glass Christmas tree ornament.

Like the air you are breathing, the Titanian atmosphere is dominated by nitrogen gas. The air pressure at the surface is 50 percent greater than at sea level on Earth, and the atmosphere is five times as deep as Earth's. Methane vapor, which accounts for at least 6 percent of the lower cloud decks' composition, might condense out as droplets, falling down to the surface as cold rain and creating actual rivers, lakes, or seas of liquid methane. Swept by a sleet of frozen hydrocarbons, Titan's "lakes" exist near the triple point for methane, which means that they may evaporate into nonexistence during long, dry periods, or that they may freeze over when the termperature drops. If there are mountains on Titan, their peaks may be capped with methane snow—glaciers of methane that flow groundward and become rivers of methane. Methane possibly plays the same role on Titan that water plays on Earth: vapor, rain, snow, slush, and ice.

More than 70 kilometers above the ground, in the thick orange haze that covers Titan, *Voyager 1* detected traces of methane, ethane (H_3C-CH_3), ethene ($H_2C = CH_2$: also called ethylene), ethyne ($HC \equiv CH$: also called acetylene), and propane ($CH_3-CH_2-CH_3$). More exotic

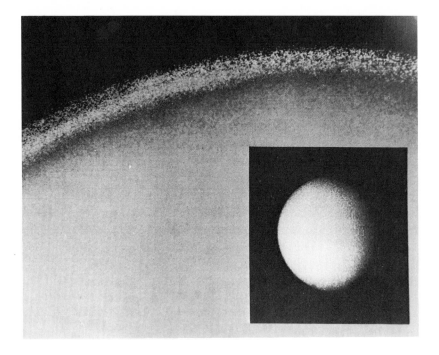

Saturn's largest moon, Titan, is the only ice world known to possess an atmosphere. The Titanian atmosphere is dominated by nitrogen, with about 6 percent methane composition and as much as 12 percent argon. Surface pressure reaches 1.5 times air pressure at sea level on Earth. Surface temperatures (about $-180°C$) are near the triple point for methane, which means that methane may play the same role on Titan that water plays on Earth: vapor, rain, and ice. This pair of photos was taken by *Voyager 1* on November 12, 1980. *Provided through the courtesy of National Aeronautics and Space Administration, California Institute of Technology, Jet Propulsion Laboratories.*

organic compounds, like formaldehyde (H_2CO) and hydrogen cyanide (HCN), also appear to be dispersed through the cloudtops. In spite of the fact that these molecules can provide the pathway for all the biology we are familiar with here on Earth, it is now too painfully clear that the lakes of Titan are too cold to support the life-building processes that could weave them together into more elaborate entities such as viruses. The methane lakes, if they exist, are so frigid that carbon dioxide and water—things we are used to breathing and drinking—are present everywhere as solid matter. They have become the rocks and sand we would find on a Titanian beach.

Titan, with a favorable combination of low gravity and dense atmosphere, is one of the most accessible bodies in the solar system for exploration by robot spacecraft. Shown here is a robot heliprobe conducting a gadabout exploration of grooved terrain similar to that seen on Jupiter's moon Ganymede. Titan is 9.54 times farther from the sun than Earth and is bathed in light nearly 100 times dimmer (approximating the brightness of a small room lit by a fluorescent lamp). Saturn itself is not visible through the moon's multilayer haze. At the surface, methane rivers might chart meandering courses down beds of hydrocarbon "snow." *Illustration and heliprobe design concept by C. R. Pellegrino.*

Possibly, we are directing too much attention at the outer skin of worlds like Titan and Ganymede, when in fact we should be drawing up plans for seismic studies to determine the nature of their interiors.

The *Voyager* missions have revealed several Jovian and Saturnian

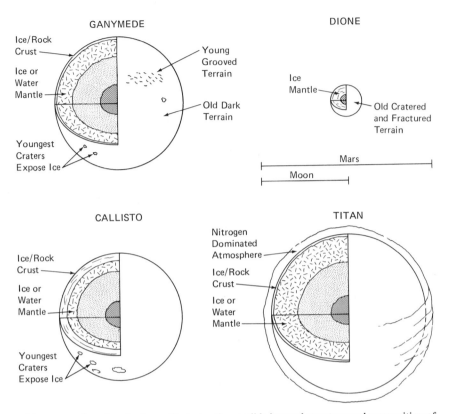

GANYMEDE

Ice/Rock Crust

Ice or Water Mantle

Youngest Craters Expose Ice

Young Grooved Terrain

Old Dark Terrain

DIONE

Ice Mantle

Old Cratered and Fractured Terrain

Mars

Moon

CALLISTO

Ice/Rock Crust

Ice or Water Mantle

Youngest Craters Expose Ice

TITAN

Nitrogen Dominated Atmosphere

Ice/Rock Crust

Ice or Water Mantle

This quartet of sectioned spheres illustrates the possible internal structure and composition of Ganymede and Callisto (Jupiter), and Dione and Titan (Saturn). The crust and mantle schematics for Ganymede and Callisto are based upon models compiled by *Voyager* scientist Torrence Johnson. According to these schematics, all four ice worlds possess differentiated rocky interiors. The ages of surface features can be partly determined by their relative darkness. Newer craters, gouged out by asteroid impacts, expose white subsurface ice. Over thousands of centuries, a constant world-wide rain of dust and marble-sized particles darkens the ice. Diameters of the moon (3600 km) and Mars (6758 km) are drawn for scale.

moons as virtual ice worlds. Eight of them—Ganymede and Callisto (which circle Jupiter) and Mimas, Enceladus, Tethys, Dione, Rhea, and Titan (which circle Saturn)—may contain more than 50 percent water by weight. Since surface temperatures never exceed a noontime high of $-148°$ C ($-297°$ F) on any of these bodies, water will not be lost by heating, liquification, and boiling away into space, as it is in the case of our moon, for example, whose rocks are disappointingly low in water and other volitiles. (Remote sensing equipment erected at the *Apollo 11* landing site did detect traces of water vapor on the moon, which caused a great deal of excitement and led briefly to theories about lunar geysers, until it was learned that urine bags left behind by the astronauts were bursting and spewing their contents.)

Apparently, Titan, Ganymede, and the other ice worlds, at least during their early histories, possessed warm interiors. Evidence from meteorites suggests that even small, asteroid-sized bodies once attained internal temperatures as high as 2,000° C, primarily through the decay of relatively short-lived radioactive elements. Radiogenic heat production would itself have been sufficient to keep the cores of the Jovian and Saturnian satellites quite hot throughout the first 500 million years of their existence; and ordinary geothermal pressures, combined with varying degrees of tidal friction occurring between sister satellites and their respective planets, might have slowed down or even prevented the cooling of their rocky interiors. (The potential for tidal friction as a heat source was demonstrated remarkably well by the volcanic eruptions seen on Io in 1979.) In essence, then, each of these ice worlds once contained a boundary area between the molten core and the frozen crust; it was a zone measured in perhaps tens of kilometers, wherein temperatures ranged between the freezing and boiling points of water. Exactly how long these warm, intermediate layers endured remains a debatable subject and, like it or not, the question is going to be with us for many years.

Analysis of *Voyager 1* and *2* images provides possible clues that the crusts of the two largest Jovian moons, Ganymede and Callisto, remained soft for several hundred million years after their formation, but that they cooled and solidified rapidly (as a continental plate measures time) to substantial depths. Current models suggest that the ice mantles of Ganymede and Callisto are hundreds, perhaps a thousand or more, kilometers deep. Assuming warm interiors, there exists a clear possibility that subterranean seas still reside within either or both of these worlds.

Of the two, only Ganymede, the larger, shows any signs of "recent" internal activity (convection or something close to it), manifested as continent-sized grooves, shifts, and breaks in its crust. By comparison, the surfaces of Callisto, whose disk is only 8.11 percent narrower, and the Saturnian moon Dione, which measures a little more than one-fifth the diameter of Ganymede, appear older; this in-

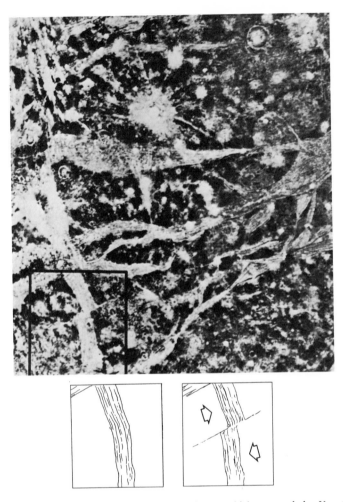

Ganymede is the largest of Jupiter's moons. This picture, which was made by *Voyager 1* at a distance of 246,000 kilometers (158,400 miles) shows an area about 1000 kilometers (620 miles) across. Ganymede's crust consists mostly of ice, which is darkest in the oldest regions. In the area shown here, much of the heavily cratered dark crust has been replaced by younger systems of mountain-sized grooves. The boxed area shows breakage and subsequent drift of a portion of Ganymede's crust, located to the southwest of a dark feature known as "the fish." *Provided through the courtesy of National Aeronautics and Space Administration, California Institute of Technology, Jet Propulsion Laboratories.*

dicates that they retained their warmth for a considerably shorter time. Indeed, the interior of Dione must have frozen clear through to its very center more than 3.5 billion years ago.

Tethys and Dione, two ice worlds with diameters of approximately 1100 kilometers (685 miles), pose in front of Saturn. The shadows of Saturn's rings and Tethys (the innermost of the two satellites) are cast onto the cloud tops. *Provided through the Courtesy of National Aeronautics and Space Administration, California Institute of Technology, Jet Propulsion Laboratories.*

Strange as the idea may seem at first glance, the same principle regulating how far a crab can stray from water also dictates whether or not water may reside inside any of the ice worlds. As objects of the same shape become larger, be they crabs or planets, volumes increase faster than surface areas; hence, young crabs, with their high ratio of surface area to volume, quickly evaporate water through their shells and can not venture as far ashore as their older, larger compatriots.

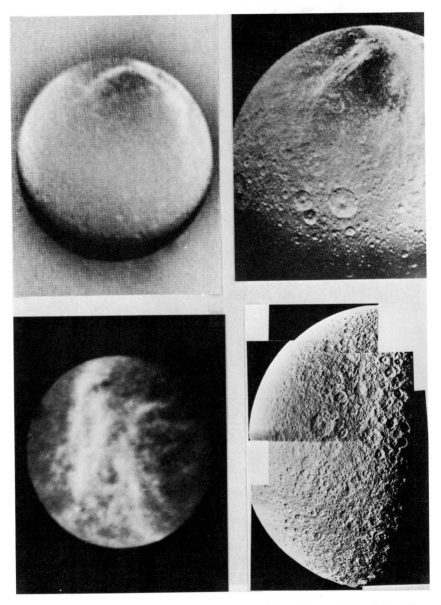

Dione (*top*) and Rhea (*bottom*), two of the large icy satellites of Saturn, display light, whispy markings on their surfaces. Shock fractures may have expelled subsurface liquid water into the cold vacuum of space where it condensed and fell as snow. Dione (*top left*) has a light background because it is seen in transit against Saturn. *Provided through the courtesy of National Aeronautics and Space Administration, California Institute of Technology, Jet Propulsion Laboratories.*

Table 8-1

	ORBITAL RADIUS (KM)	DIAMETER (KM)	DENSITY (GM/CM³)	ALBEDO
JUPITER				
Io	421,600	3,640	3.5	20%
Europa	670,900	3,130	3.0	60%
Ganymede	1,070,000	5,270	1.9	50%
Callisto	1,880,000	4,840	1.8	50%
SATURN				
Mimas	185,400	390	1.2	60%
Enceladus	238,200	500	1.1	100%
Tethys	294,600	1,050	1.0	80%
Dione	377,400	1,120	1.4	60%
Rhea	526,800	1,530	1.2	60%
Titan	1,222,000	5,118	1.9+	19%
Hyperion	1,482,000	310	—	30%
Iapetus	3,562,000		1.2	3% and 50%

Characteristics summary of some Jovian and Saturnian satellites.

Dione, as a small world, has a high ratio of surface to volume, and it radiates internal heat into space far more rapidly than a body five or ten times its own girth. Thus, small worlds solidify faster and to substantially greater depths than large worlds.

And there is Titan, almost identical to Ganymede in bulk composition and density (approximately 1.9 grams per cubic centimeter), and nearly 2.5 percent smaller in diameter; yet it is the only ice world known to have an atmosphere. (It is possible that the large satellite of Neptune, Triton, is both larger and heavier than Titan and that its surface may be covered by a world-wide ocean of liquid nitrogen.) Titan, residing almost twice as far from the sun as Ganymede, is exposed to a much weaker solar wind. This has permitted its gravitational field to capture and maintain a permanent hold on gases accreted during its birth stages and, to a lesser degree, vented out through its mantle. If we could strip away Titan's atmosphere and make its surface visible, we would probably see a craterless, weather-beaten version of Ganymede's grooved terrain, marked here and there, perhaps, by a volcanic extrusion of water ice. "The bizarre," observed one *Voyager* scientist, "has become the commonplace." Think upon that. We are looking at worlds whose lava is water, and we are about to contemplate life in those seas of molten ice.

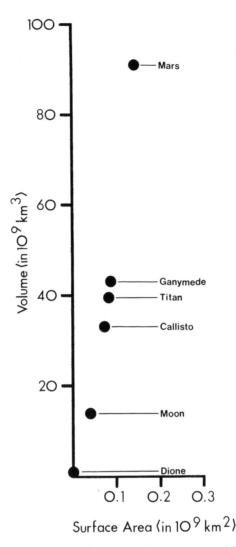

Surface areas and volumes of Mars, the moon, and some Jovian and Saturnian satellites. The proportion of surface area, through which internal heat can be radiated away into space, decreases relative to volume as radius increases. Thus, the Earth, with a surface area of 0.509 billion square kilometers and a volume of 607 billion cubic kilometers, is molten almost throughout. Mars, with a greater ratio of surface to volume has a thicker, less pliable crust, and what we see as continental drift on Earth is expressed as a volcano 27 kilometers (17 miles) high and a canyon system that girdles two-thirds of the planet. Ganymede is the only ice world known, in the absence of tidal flexing, to have grooved terrain suggestive of tectonic activity, while Callisto, with a radius only 210 kilometers smaller, lacks any hints of such features.

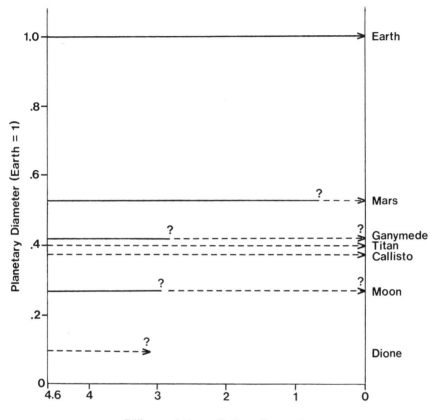

Billions of Years Before Present

The duration of a planet's or a satellite's molten interior, assuming the absence of tidal flexing or other heat sources, is rooted simply in the size of the body. Solid lines (*left*) indicate evidence of surface volcanism or tectonic activity. Dotted lines indicate the possible duration of molten interiors. An approximate date for the cessation of volcanism of Mars' surface can be estimated from a count of meteorite craters on top of lava flows. The youngest volcanic rocks brought back from the moon crystallized approximately 2.8 billion years ago. Although the ascent of lava through the crust ceased by that time, the moon may still possess a molten interior. The ice worlds should not have experienced any significant surface volcanism. Ice is a very good insulator, able to trap heat and prevent its radiation into space. Nevertheless, bodies as small as Dione and Rhea (with diameters of 1120 and 1530 km respectively) should have frozen through to the core more than 3 billion years ago.

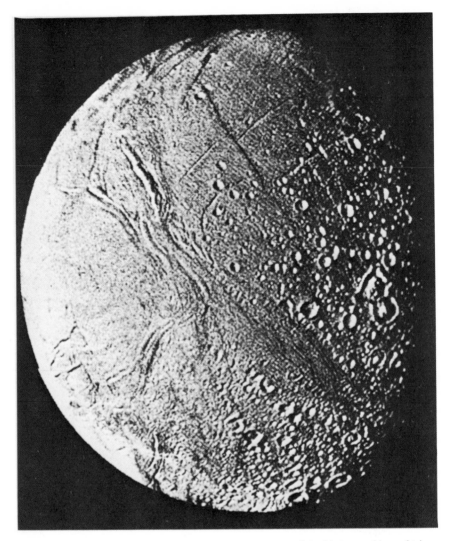

Enceladus, viewed from *Voyager 2,* is a 500 kilometer (310 mile) wide ice world caught in a gravitational tug-of-war between Saturn and two other satellites, Tethys and Dione (Enceladus sweeps past Tethys at only one-sixth the distance separating Earth from the moon). Tidal flexing has dumped enormous loads of frictional energy into Enceladus's interior, warming the water-ice, fracturing the crust, and triggering the formation of Ganymede-like grooved terrain that has obliterated ancient crater fields. Enceladus is a remarkably active ice world, but not too active: It has not, like the Jovian moons Io and Europa, vented all or most of its volatiles into space. With a density of 1.1 (water has a density of 1.0), Enceladus must possess a rock core measuring no more than a few tens of kilometers across—a world within a world—overlaid, possibly, by an ocean of liquid water with a self-sealing icy shell. Because of its small size and

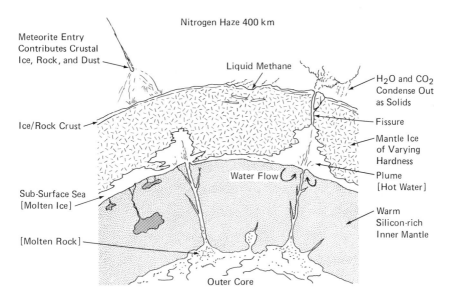

Hydrothermal activity inside Titan is shown schematically (not to scale) as it might have appeared about 3 billion years ago. Venting through fractures in the ice mantle (nearly 1000 km thick), if it occurred at all, would have been infrequent.

Clearly, the ice worlds circling Jupiter and Saturn did at one time contain subsurface seas, many of them throughout the first half billion years of their history. During that same time period on Earth, our remotest ancestors—colloidal droplets with primitive catalytic abilities—appeared in the oceans, and protocell evolution commenced, culminating after some 700 million years (probably much earlier) in the development of a genetic apparatus.

Evidently, a similar if not identical drama was being acted out in the ancient, subterranean seas of Titan, Ganymede, and even little Dione. If warm, intermediate layers have persisted above the outer cores of any of these satellites (and that is an important if), then preliving

---

low gravity, temperatures and pressures in Enceladus's subsurface seas (if such still exist) may closely parallel those found on Earth's abyssal plains. Current estimates of the rate of tidal heating in Enceladus suggest that internal water must have a melting point somewhat lower than that of pure water ice and may therefore be mixed with methane clathrates and/or hydrates of ammonia (as water in our oceans contains salt). *Photo courtesy of National Aeronautics and Space Administration, California Institute of Technology, Jet Propulsion Laboratories.*

chemical evolution should have long since matured into genetic evolution. If one is permitted to speculate on this result, it is possible that advanced multicellular life resides near Jupiter and Saturn.

In appearance, such creatures might look eerily familiar, being shaped by physical laws similar to those governing the forms of animals dwelling on the dark abyssal plains of terrestrial oceans. One can easily imagine a sea populated by fast-swimming, torpedo-shaped, fish-like animals possessing fins and gills in just the right places. Conceivably, they would share the waters with other fauna reminiscent of earthly phyla, including minute pelagic Crustacea, jellyfish, and nautilus-like mollusks; but familiar as they may seem, a "fish" inhabiting the mantle of a Saturnian moon would, in terms of ancestry, be no more related to a barracuda than a barracuda is to a Venus-flytrap.

The subsurface environment will dictate other major differences between life in its seas and that on Earth. Our own deep-sea fishes tend to spend at least portions of their lives in a sun-lit nursery ground near the surface; and at great depths they are surrounded by flashes of living light. Thus, large light-gathering eyes are useful to them, whereas the interior of Titan or one of its companions is not likely to provide any meaningful illumination. Creatures living therein might lack eyes and color, like cave dwelling crustaceans and fishes known here on Earth, and they would "see" their surroundings as odors and faint disturbances in the water—even bioelectric impulses coursing through the muscles of prey and predator species. (The emergence of bioluminescence, however, could open up myriad possibilities.)

A hypothetical Titanian "fish" will live in an environment of such tremendous pressure, exerted by many kilometers of overlaying ice, that transferral even to the deepest reaches of the Atlantic Ocean could not prevent the cells of its body from exploding like tiny bombshells. Indeed, the "fish" itself might rupture with sufficient force to maim or kill passersby.

Molecular biologists may well be concerned with the effects of extreme pressure on the large molecules of living organisms; and the special biochemistries that are possible in those warm, dark recesses remain open to broad speculation. Photosynthesis, for example, can not be conducted in the absence of light. Nevertheless, a substitute metabolic pathway has recently been discovered right here on Earth. Appropriately enough, the process (called chemosynthesis) is occur-

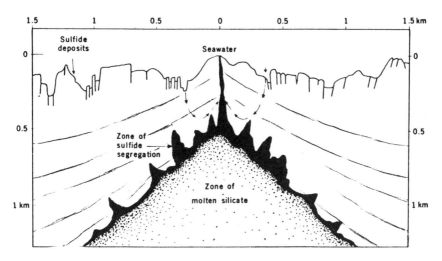

Hydrothermal activity on the Galápagos Rift in the East Pacific is shown schematically. The illustration shows the axial zone of a rapidly spreading (5 cm per year) ridge. Seawater penetrates into block-faulted areas and is expelled near the spreading center. *Reprinted from Science, vol. 207, pp. 1433–1444, 28 March 1980. Copyright 1980 by the American Association for the Advancement of Science.*

ring in bacteria living near volcanic hot-water springs on the Galapagos Rift, located some 2.5 kilometers (1.6 miles) under the Pacific Ocean. Protruding from the bottom like organ pipes, hydrothermal vents spout continuous jets of hot water laden with sulfur compounds, silicates, and an assortment of heavier elements such as iron, copper, and zinc. The bacteria are able to slowly burn or oxidize hydrogen sulfide (H_2S) emitted by the vents, using it as a source of energy almost in the same way that green plants use energy provided by the sun. Like plants, the bacteria direct this energy toward the splitting of carbon dioxide into separate carbon and oxygen atoms (reduction). They then "steal" the carbon atoms, linking them together to form carbohydrates (fixation) and liberating oxygen as a by-product. Around them, the ocean floor becomes an oasis, supporting dense communities of clams, limpets, giant tube-building worms, barnacles, crabs, and an occasional eel-like fish, with the carbohydrate-producing bacteria forming the base of the food chain.*

---

* At least one hydrothermal-vent tube worm, *Rifta pachyptila,* does not feed on chemosynthetic bacteria but is itself a chemosynthetic organism. Its tissues carry enzymes able to catalyze synthesis of the energy-storing molecule adenosine triphosphate (ATP) from adenosine

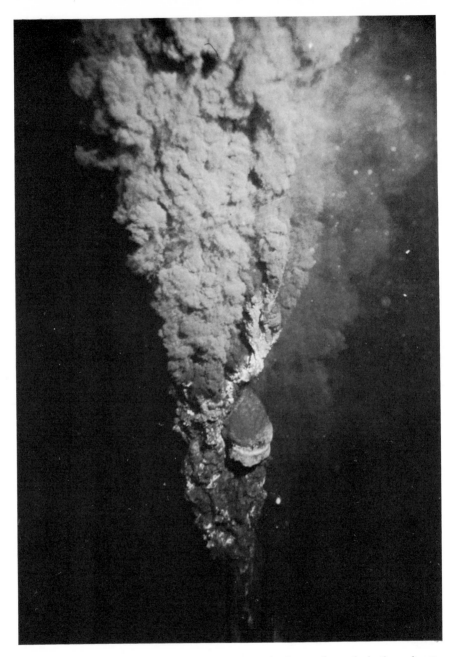

Water heated to four times its boiling temperature at sea level spurts from a hydrothermal vent on the Galápagos Rift. This photograph was taken at a depth of 2.6 kilometers (1.6 miles) by the submersible *Alvin* during Expedition Rise. *Courtesy of D. Foster, R. Ballard, and the RISE Project Group, Woods Hole, Massachusetts.*

The imagination is rarely more forcefully awakened than when one considers the hellish temperatures at which water is emanating from the Galapagos springs. It seems most inconceivable that water heated to four times its boiling point at sea level, ranging between 300° and 410° C (572° and 770° F), should create an oasis. The superheated water is permitted to exist in liquid form simply because, at a depth of 2.5 kilometers (about 1.6 miles), the ocean presses in every direction at once with a force exceeding 250 times that of the air you are now breathing. That may not sound like a great deal of pressure, but if we were to transport you to one of the Galapagos hot-water springs, your whole body would be compressed instantly to the size of a baseball. Hence, water exiting from the chimney-shaped vents does not boil, even at 500° C; and we, as observers, can not help but wonder to what extent high pressure might counteract the destructive effects of high temperature on biochemical systems. Although the venting water does not seem to come into direct contact with the community it supports (as suggested by the presence of chimney-top-dwelling worms and crabs that, mere centimeters from the spouts, appear to be bathed in relatively cooler water), life on the Galapagos springs may exist at higher temperatures than anywhere else on Earth. A single sample of water from a vent did not contain any bacteria; but that one sample is all we have to read from, and the answers to many new and exciting questions about extreme pressure-temperature biology, whether we are talking about the inside of Titan or the bottom of the Pacific Ocean, must await further investigation of our own planet.

Looking outward from our Earth, peering down through the skin of a Saturnian moon, we are reminded, perhaps, that Charles Darwin's "warm little pond"—the pools and rivers of a terrestrial globe—may not be a universal and invariable requirement for the development of life.

---

diphosphate (ADP) by using reducing power generated by the oxidation of sulfur compounds, especially hydrogen sulfide (H_2S), that emanates from the vents. Other enzymes use the energy generated by sulfur oxidation to reduce and fix carbon dioxide, releasing oxygen as a by-product. This first example of an animal that synthesizes its own food like a plant—almost an alien in our seas—lacks a mouth and digestive system. Preliminary evidence suggests that *R. pachyptila's* chemosynthetic abilities might have evolved from a symbiosis of chemosynthetic bacteria with its own cells.

9
Fire and Rain

The heavens call to you, and circle around you, displaying to you their eternal splendors, and your eye gazes only to Earth

Dante

The world, although well-lighted with fluorescents and incandescent bulbs and neon, is still full of odd dark corners and unsettling nooks and crannies.

Stephen King

Hell's Gate (New Zealand's hydrothermal wasteland), I think, is the most damnable place I have ever visited, and I'd willingly have paid ten pounds not to have seen it.

George Bernard Shaw

The dryness of Earth is a puzzle. Through the eyes of *Voyagers 1* and *2* we have seen Ganymede and Titan, giant orbiting snowbanks containing as much as 60 percent water by weight. Even the Murchison meteorite, with a 10 percent water composition when it arrived in Australia, came from somewhere that is 2,000 times wetter than the Earth itself. Which is something one has to stop and think about for a moment.

All the water in the oceans, lakes, rivers, and atmosphere, if spread uniformly over the surface of the Earth, would form a layer almost 2.5 kilometers (approximately 1.5 miles) deep. True, this is enough water to erase all traces of human habitation on our planet; but across the 12,732-kilometer (7,913-mile) diameter of the Earth, it barely qualifies as a paper-thin membrane. If, for analogy, you were to hold a polished brass sphere about the size of a basketball in your hands and then puff just a single breath of air onto it, the amount of water vapor condensed on its surface would be comparatively greater than the Pacific, Atlantic, Arctic, and Indian Oceans combined. And the moon is drier still.

Why are the Earth and moon so different from their compatriots in the outer solar system? We may be tempted to imagine a presolar nebula of varying composition; but the whole solar system, as far as we can tell, seems to have been created from roughly the same ingredients. The answer must therefore lie in our nearness to the sun.

If you could steal Titan and place it in orbit as a second moon around Earth, its atmosphere would blow away almost instantly. Then its icy mountains would melt and boil, their vapors trailing away from the sun and blazing so brightly across our skies that even by daylight the wisps of Titan would provide a spectacle more lovely than a hundred Halley's comets put together. Several years later, Titan will have shrunk to a bundle of dry rocks only slightly larger than our moon. The Earth, by comparison, is large enough to maintain a hold on its gaseous and liquid volatiles, at least at a distance of 150 million kilometers (93 million miles) from the sun; but closer, transported, say, to the orbit of Mercury, our thin shell of air and water would vanish almost immediately.

The sun ignited between 4.5 and 4.6 billion years ago, a time during which the Earth and moon were growing ever-fatter under an unceasing shower of rock and rock-ice. In the absence of a solar wind, the two bodies might have acquired atmospheres consisting largely of accreted gases and impact-generated vapors. The presolar Earth and moon would have developed hot, liquid interiors very quickly. The energy necessary for the initial melting is likely to have been provided by the potential energy of accretion and gravitational compaction, especially if (as appears to be the case) the greater part of their mass accumulated rapidly—within several thousands or even hundreds of centuries—so that very large quantities of potential energy were not radiated away into space, but instead became trapped in their interiors. Heavy elements such as nickel, iron, gold, iridium, and particle-emitting metals—originally distributed over the volumes of both planets—began to sink toward their cores. Radioactive elements became concentrated within smaller volumes, triggering more melting. Ice liquified and flowed toward the surface. Oceans overlain by icy crusts might have formed, producing approximate likenesses of Europa, Ganymede, or Titan. Meanwhile, the meteoritic bombardment continued.

From observations of very young stars in various stages of formation, we now know that the onset of hydrogen-fusion burning blasts an enormous amount of gas away from a star's surface and immediate surroundings. This blast is called a *T-Tauri Wind*. It is similar to the solar wind produced by particles (protons and electrons, mostly) shed from our sun's surface today, but it is many times more powerful—a gale by comparison. With the ignition of our sun came heat and light. If the moon did possess plains and mountain ranges of ice, these would have steamed; but the vapor never condensed into thunderclouds or returned as rain. As the T-Tauri Wind raged across the surface, all gases and liquids were stripped away. The outward pressure was so powerful that the inner planets—Mercury, Venus, Earth, the moon, and Mars—were cleansed of their primordial atmospheres.

Rocks collected from the moon by the *Apollo* and *Luna* missions, combined with seismic studies conducted by the *Apollo* crews* have provided glimpses of what happened next: The daughter decay products of radioactive elements have dated the last extensive heating and melting, as indicated by the oldest rocks found on the lunar surface, to about 4.2 billion years ago, suggesting that the moon's crust had rigidified by that time. By 3.9 billion years ago, the great storm of meteoritic bombardment had begun to subside, and massive asteroids had excavated the mare basins, puncturing the skin on the Earth-facing side. Between 3.3 and 3.8 billion years ago, basaltic lava welled up from inside and slowly filled the wounds, forming the dark lunar maria or "seas." Then, as radioactive elements continued to decay, and their abundance dwindled, internal heating failed to keep pace with cooling at the surface. The crust solidified to a depth of nearly 1,000 kilometers (622 miles) and became impenetrable to ascending lava. By 3.2 billion years ago, volcanic activity at the surface had

---

* The lunar modules, having performed their tasks, were jettisoned and crash-landed on the surface. Seismic sensors, planted by the astronauts, recorded the commotion in the moon's crust and beamed it to Earth.

Many stars shown in this region of gas and dust (called NGC 2264) in the constellation Monoceros are only now beginning hydrogen fusion-burning. Several members of this stellar nursery are presently in the T-Tauri stage, producing such powerful stellar winds that any inner, rocky planets (if such exist) must now be stripped of their atmospheres. *Courtesy of Hale Observatories.*

Between 3.3 and 3.8 billion years ago, oceans of lava welled up from within the moon and slowly filled the mare basins to form the flat lunar lowlands. This view across the Sea of Tranquility was photographed by the *Apollo 8* crew. The raised rims of flooded craters are visible at the bottom right. Sharply defined craters with bowl-shaped bottoms (like the two seen at the bottom left) are the result of subsequent impacts on top of the solidified lava field. *Courtesy of NASA's Johnson Space Center, Houston, Texas.*

Seen from lunar orbit in *Apollo 16,* the western edge of Mare Cognitum (the Known Sea) lies pooled at the feet of the Montes Riphaeus highlands. The smaller craters visible on the lava field are approximately one kilometer across. *Courtesy of NASA's Johnson Space Center, Houston, Texas.*

ended. Except for several million new craters, we view the moon today much as it looked then.

If the moon was hot very early in its history, the Earth, with its greater volume and relatively smaller ratio of surface area, must have been even hotter. The planet was dominated by volcanism and the

Geologist-astronaut Harrison Schmitt working beside a boulder on the lunar highlands. The boulder, half buried in lunar dust, was ejected by a distant asteroid impact long before dinosaurs appeared on Earth and has lain undisturbed on the moon's surface ever since. The prow of the lunar roving vehicle is visible on the right. *Courtesy of NASA's Johnson Space Center, Houston, Texas.*

outgassing of volatile compounds such as steam, carbon dioxide, carbon monoxide, hydrogen sulfide, and possibly methane. Vast quantities of nitrogen gas, and some hydrogen and sulfur dioxide, were probably also vented from the Earth. These gave rise to an atmosphere bearing little resemblance to Haldane, Oparin, Miller and Urey's hydrogen-rich, highly reducing recipe for the origin of life. Many geochemists believe that the Jupiter-like primordial atmosphere —lingering residues of the presolar nebula—either never existed or vanished with the T Tauri Wind. The 3.76-billion-year-old rocks from Isua, Greenland, are in support of this hypothesis. James Walker of the University of Michigan has found them to contain carbonate (CO_3) minerals, which he concludes could only have formed if the atmospheric carbon was, at that time, predominantly carbon dioxide rather than methane. His current model calls for an atmosphere deficient in oxygen and composed largely of molecular nitrogen (N_2), with concentrations of carbon dioxide that were at near present-day levels.*

Evidence for an early atmosphere being released from within the Earth has begun to cause unrest among molecular biologists, forcing a reevaluation of experiments involving electrical discharges through methane and ammonia gas over water. We know that the primitive Earth had many energy sources acting upon its surface. Ruptures in the crust were present everywhere, both as laval outflows and hydrothermal vents. The sky was clouded with steam and volcanic dust, which descended as torrential rains and lightning. Rivers of lava flowed into leaping, hissing water, and the decay of radioactive elements produced enough surface radiation to cause sickness in humans. Into this land—evil in appearance and barren—fell the meteors. Pebbles and chips of ice struck the atmosphere, burning and flashing and trailing smoke above the clouds. Boulders streaked down, impacting, their shock waves blending undetectably with the terrestrial din.

Then, as now, there was sunlight; but the upper atmosphere did not contain great amounts of oxygen (this would have to await the emergence of photosynthetic cells), which was needed to absorb much of the sun's ultraviolet radiation to form an ozone (O_3) layer impenetrable to short-wave (high-energy) ultraviolet light. Most of the ultraviolet rays pierced clear through to the ground, providing the dominant (and most exploitable) form of energy input.

Given this physical setting, we must next ask whether or not chemical evolution could have gotten a start from photochemical and

---

*Thomas Gold, director of the Center for Radiophysics and Space Research at Cornell University, has presented convincing arguments that methane gas could have formed in deep layers of the Earth's crust by the heating of carbon-containing meteoritic debris. Like grease in an oven, organic matter contained in carbonaceous chrondrites might have broken down into liquids and gases. Or the carbon itself, heated with water, might have made methane.

Science editor Philip J. Abelson has argued in favor of a primitive atmosphere that resembled today's minus all its oxygen. To prove his point, he showed that methane in an oxygen-deficient atmosphere should have reacted chemically to form carbon deposits, which did not seem to be present in rocks of early Precambrian age. More recently, Bartholomew Nagy and his team at the University of Arizona found 3.76-billion-year-old rocks from southwestern Greenland to contain thin veins of carbon (graphite); they attribute these to the reaction of methane gas with iron oxides, which oxidized the methane to graphite and reduced the iron oxides to ferrous-ferric oxide (magnetite). If Gold's hypothesis for subsurface methane production is correct, the methane source could have been local steam vents.

Hydrothermal vent activity on New Zealand's North Island. Gases emitted by the vents include hydrogen sulfide (H_2S), sulfur dioxide (SO_2), carbon dioxide (CO_2), and traces of methane (CH_4). *Photos by C. R. Pellegrino.*

thermal interactions with an atmosphere that was possibly only mildly reducing.

As early as 1966, when methane-ammonia models held center stage, Philip J. Abelson was generating amino acids from mixtures of nitrogen gas, carbon monoxide, carbon dioxide, and hydrogen. the principal organic product was hydrogen cyanide (HCN), and this was formed (not unexpectedly) only when hydrogen was present. In more recent work, Clair Folsome, Andrew Brittain, and NASA biologists Sherwood Chang and Adolph Smith passed electrical discharges through an atmosphere of molecular nitrogen over water laced with mixtures of calcium carbonate ($CaCO_3$) and reduced iron (i.e., iron not bound with oxygen, and therefore able to act as an "oxygen scavenger"). Among the products were high yields of hydrazine (H_2NNH_2) and carbohydrazides ($H_2NNHCONHNH_2$). These were produced after only ten hours of spark discharge and could serve as reactive organic molecules for further chemical evolution. Significantly, they were produced in the absence of methane, ammonia, and molecular hydrogen (H_2). In a similar study, John Or'o of the University of Houston passed electrical discharges through a mixture of carbon monoxide and nitrogen gas over water. He reports the recovery of amino acids and two major nucleic acid bases, adenine and guanine (although the yields were unimpressively low).

If the geochemists are right about a mildly reducing atmosphere, the classic Oparin-Haldane "primordial soup" is more likely to have been a very dilute broth. There is no complete answer yet, but underlying all this is the fact that under any form of energy input (even bouncing a flask of carbon, nitrogen, hydrogen, and oxygen off a wall for several hours), and almost irrespective of whether conditions happen to be mildly or highly reducing, complex organic compounds are produced. And they are produced from some of the most abundant elements found on the surface of this planet.

Fred Hoyle, Chandra Wickramasinghe, and many other investigators would like to do without a primordial soup entirely. With comets mopping up masses of interstellar material and condensing it onto layers of ice and dust, prebiological organic molecules may eventually comprise as much as 30 percent of a comet's mass. When a comet approaches the inner planets, heat from the sun warms the ice, churning the organic slush and polymerizing methane, formaldehyde, and hydrogen cyanide into more elaborate structures. We know from spectroscopic analyses, conducted by the *Skylab* astronauts in 1974, that the comet Kohoutek contains amino acids and circular organic compounds. Hoyle extrapolates from this, suggesting that comets became sites for the synthesis of protein droplets, porphyrin molecules, protocells, and, ultimately, chlorophyll and life itself. Then, about 4.0 billion years ago, direct collisions with comets carried the first living organisms into our seas: seeds waiting to take root on a friendly shore.

While comets, asteroids, and meteorites undoubtedly contributed water, minerals, and organic compounds to the Earth (and continue to do so today), it seems implausible that there exists any specific molecule or series of molecules required for the origin of life that can be manufactured *only* in outer space. Considering the ease with which prebiological molecules can be derived from simpler compounds, there is no reason on Earth why our planet should not have been able to cook up life in its own seas, which had one very important advantage over asteroids and comets: *surface tension on water.* At the surface of a pond, where oily films and fine dusts gather, lies a remarkable binding and mixing medium—a medium that would not have been present inside Phobos, Ceres, Titan, Enceladus, or Kohoutek.

Carl Sagan's cosmic calendar portrays the history of the universe as a single year, with the Earth forming on or about September 14, dinosaurs arriving on Christmas Eve, and human civilization occupying the last few seconds of December 31. We have just entered the new year, equipped with brains and seeking to understand how we were made. Our bodies ripple with energy releasing and capturing molecules that conduct symphonies written on DNA and performed by protein. The music might have begun, at one time or another, on an Earth laid bare—dry as an old bone—under the fire of a very young sun. It begins to look as if the composer in our lives was the Earth itself, in whose exalations and regurgitations the first cells developed. Don't you see it? The poets were right all along. We live, every one of us, on the surface of a parent, not just on a planet.

10
Punctuated What?

As for your doctrine, I am prepared to go to the stake for it. I am prepared to go to the stake, if requisite, in support of chapter 9, and most parts of chapters 10, 11, and 12. As for the rest, you have loaded yourself with an unnecessary difficulty in adopting Natura non facit saltum (*nature does not make leaps*) *so unreservedly.*

Thomas Huxley
(in a letter to Charles Darwin)

We didn't need "Roots" to remind us that genealogy exerts a strange fascination over people. If uncovering the traces of a distant great-grandparent in a small overseas village fills us with satisfaction, then probing further back to an African ape, a reptile, a fish, that still-unknown ancestor of vertebrates, a single-celled forbear, and even the origin of life itself can be awesome. Unfortunately, the further back we go the more fascinated we become and the less we know.

Stephen Jay Gould

The oldest known rocks on Earth protrude from under the Greenland ice cap approximately 150 kilometers (93 miles) northeast of Godthåb. They are moderately metamorphosed sediments, dating back to almost 3.8 billion years ago; and oil immersion microscopy has revealed that these sediments have spherical and ovoid globules embedded in narrow veins of graphite. The microstructures are themselves composed of graphite, occurring as aggregates and only occasionally dispersed through the mineral matrix. They range between 5

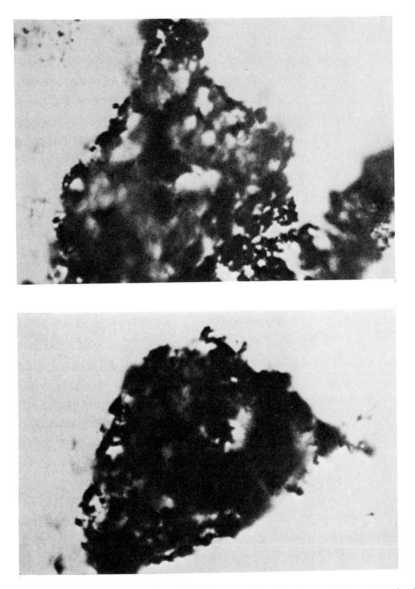

These microstructures were found in 3.76 billion year old sedimentary rocks from Greenland. The evidence suggests a nonbiological synthesis of these structures, which possibly represent the immediate precursors of living cells. Both objects have diameters of 20 μ. *Courtesy of B. Nagy.*

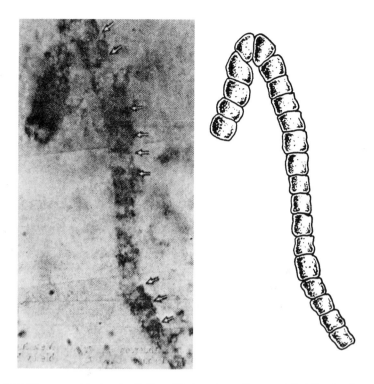

These 3.5-billion-year-old microfossils from Western Australia suggest that the step from protocell to cell was made in a geological nanosecond, almost literally as the Earth was forming from a ball of dust and gas in space. *Photos courtesy of D. I. Groves. Illustration by C. R. Pellegrino.*

and 30 microns in diameter, are morphologically simple and resemble the class one microstructures found in carbonaceous meteorites. Nagy and his co-workers suggest a nonbiological origin of the Greenland microstructures, which possibly represent the immediate precursors of living cells.

On the other side of the world, in an uninhabited corner of western Australia, distinctive mound-shaped rocks called stromatolites, which are believed to have been formed by blue-green algae (now classified as cyanobacteria) and related organisms, were discovered in 1980. They are the oldest stromatolites ever found, dating back to 3.5 billion years ago. Their existence means that only 300 million years after the Greenland sediments were laid down, true cells appeared in our seas.

Uncropped by grazing creatures such as snails, they flourished—layer upon layer—secreting lime (CaOH) as they grew; this lime accumulated to form stony, coral-like pillars and cushions.

An American-Australian team headed by University of California, Los Angeles, paleobiologist J. William Schopf, which knew from radiometric dating that the stromatolites were worth studying, cut them into thin slices and examined them microscopically. They found at least seven varieties of surprisingly complex organisms, including long multicellular filaments, which had evolved and established colonies in shallow, sun-lit waters even as the moon bled lava into its mare basins.

Surely, the first cells predated the Australian fossils. We can not guess how many millions of years earlier they appeared; but by 3.5 billion years ago, life had probably spread throughout every major body of water on Earth. This is quite a big step, from protocell to cell—a leap that made us fully alive. And it occurred in the span of less than 300 million years. (You will recall that the estimated life expectancy of Fox Holes in large asteroids is 500 million years.) The difference in complexity between a protocell and a blue-green alga (with its loops of DNA, ribosomes, membranes, systems for the regulation of water content, and molecules of chlorophyll tucked neatly into lamellae) is almost as vast as that between an alga and a man. One set of rocks shows us what appear to be protocells. Another reveals actual colonies of living cells. But what happened in between?

Ideally, we might hope to find intermediates in rocks both older than the Australian stromatolites and younger than the Greenland sediments, creatures bridging the gap between a preliving ancestor and a living descendent. Unfortunately, we will probably find older stromatolites and younger protocells, narrowing the space in which the jump was made and increasing the size of the problem. As rocks measure time, colonies of living cells simply appeared on Earth—suddenly, as though a lamp had been switched on. Then, for nearly 2.9 billion years, very little seemed to happen.

About 700 million years ago, worms began to enter the fossil record. They were followed in close succession by jellyfish, brachiopods, trilobites, and an assortment of oceanic plankton, which proliferated all over the planet. Next, multicellular plants came bursting out of the sea, with insects in hot pursuit.

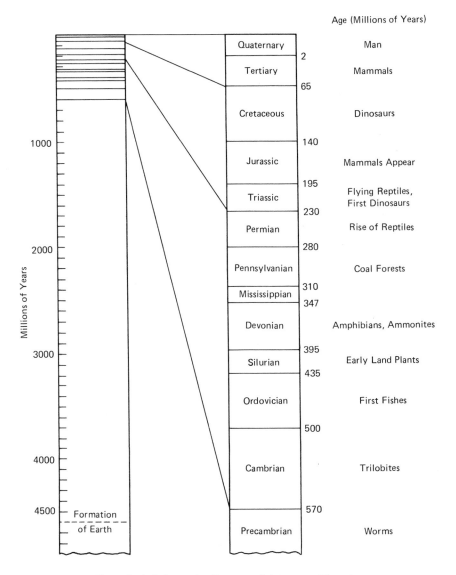

The geological time scale. *Courtesy of Astronomy Magazine.*

Even where detailed records exist, the data are often confusing. We can trace the development of a burrowing clam belonging to the genus *Anadara* over 2 million years of the Miocene epoch (approximately 12 to 21 million years ago), during which time the position of one muscle gradually shifted by 1.5 centimeters (0.5 inch). The clam then vanished from the fossil record, to be replaced by a closely related species in which the muscle had shifted abruptly by 1.5 centimeters in the opposite direction. What kind of evolution is this, which seems to explode the notion of gradual, stately change in the history of life?

The fossil record is loaded with species that appear out of nowhere (punctuation), remain unchanged throughout most of their history (stasis), and then disappear with equal speed, looking little, if at all, different from their great-grandparents. These phenomena seem, at least superficially, to suggest a fossil record that is imperfect—no, worse, a shambles. The stasis exhibited by many species over millions —often tens of millions and sometimes hundreds of millions of years (consider the horseshoe crab and the cockroach)—is ignored by many researchers as not constituting data, while sudden appearances and disappearances are attributed to a sloppy fossil record.

In an attempt to lessen the tensions between genetics and geology, Niles Eldredge of the American Museum of Natural History and Stephen Jay Gould of Harvard University introduced the model of *punctuated equilibria* in 1972. According to this model (which has its roots in Harvard systematist Ernst Mayr's *allopatric theory,* wherein new species arise in very small populations at the edges or frontiers of a species' geographic range), punctuation, or rapid change, is typically associated with small founding populations cut off from genetic communication with their parental group.

Consider the spread of European sparrows across North America. They were imported into New England during the 1850s, and the Atlantic Ocean has since prevented contact with the European population. Already, the two populations differ slightly. Sparrows inhabiting warm coastal areas in southeastern and southwestern North America tend to be small, while those living in northern inland areas, which are characterized by severe winters, are typically larger—even fat. Just as Titan, with its large ratio of volume to surface area, holds internal heat better than a smaller world with relatively greater surface area, large sparrows are better protected against freezing in cold climates. Since sparrows lose heat at the body surface, an increase in volume, and a corresponding decrease in relative surface area, helps the birds to stay warm. Consider also that the sparrows radiated from New England to California, Alaska, and Mexico in the space of a single human lifetime, establishing a new central population throughout the entire continental United States. This should give you some idea of how rapidly invasions by new species can take place.

Inland Sparrows may be larger than coastal sparrows, but they are still sparrows and genetic exchange is continuing across America (no new species are likely to evolve in Nebraska). Speciation calls for populations to establish themselves in fringe zones, say, on the Aleutian Islands. Major evolutionary change may occur in these small peripheral populations. Favorable traits can spread quickly among the isolates. Variation within the populations will serve as the raw material (and the raw material only). Natural selection will then control the direction of change, if there is to be any change. Acting on small numbers, selection tends to be more intense, setting the stage for the formation of new species. In higher latitudes, the birds will grow larger. Bill shape may alter to accommodate a broader diet of hard-to-find foods, and breeding periods may change, further isolating the birds from their ancestral group. Meanwhile, in the large central population, favorable variations can be expected to spread very slowly (mainly because they are diluted), and many of these will be contributed by the returning descendents of pioneers who had migrated to geographically marginal areas where the species could barely maintain a foothold. Small changes may occur to meet the requirements of slowly drying or cooling environments, but major genetic overhauls will be restricted to instances such as our hypothetical Aleutian population.

Let's give the Aleutian sparrows 300,000 years of isolation and then begin establishing them on the Alaskan mainland (members will also have occasionally "leaked off" the islands in the interim, but will not have established viable colonies). They are larger than their forbears, lighter colored, perhaps, with a different-shaped beak. They breed at different times. Hence, as they spread southward, they will not mate with members of the central population. What will the fossil record look like millions of years later?

We are not likely to find the Aleutian sparrows prior to their break-out onto the mainland. They are too small a group, with too few of them venturing into places where they may become fossilized. And the change occurs too quickly to be recorded in transition. But European sparrows—hundreds of them—are becoming fossilized in North America right now. We will first meet the European sparrow as a fossil when it appears everywhere at once as a large central population. Though taxonomists may ponder the longer tibiae of inland sparrows, and from them make some inference about ancient climates, we should see no major change during the population's fossil history. Then, the Aleutian sparrow, a related species with a different beak and bigger bones, invades the ancestral range, appearing suddenly and possibly even displacing the European variety. If the Aleutian sparrows become a successful central population, we will expect to see no great change in the fossils they leave behind (they will be in equilibrium) until their own peripheral isolates form new branches of the genus and radiate away from the source to establish new central populations.

Darwin saw evolution as a slow, laborious process, crawling step by sequential step, steadily, and powered by variation and selection through many generations. We have no doubt that many species arise through the accumulation of very small changes; but if the fossil record is to be taken seriously, then some, perhaps most, do not. The record does not show a gradual transformation of creatures into new forms, but instead shows species emerging in geological instants and then not altering in major ways over millions of years. The *punctuated equilibrium* model does accept the Darwinian tradition of a two-step evolutionary process, with variation producing raw material and natural selection directing (or preventing) change. The model is, fundamentally, a theory about the characteristic rate of change (the origin of new species). It addresses the dilemma of morphological constancy within successful fossil species and of abrupt replacement by descendents very different in appearance. Eldredge and Gould read the fossil record literally (as perhaps it should be read) and regard such anomalies as an expression of how evolution works when compressed into geological time.

Nature, it seems, does make leaps, sometimes giving rise to new taxa in only a few generations, perhaps even in one. Two such examples come from our own century. During the 1930s, a plague attacked a common species of marine plant life known as *Zostera,* or eel grass, almost forcing it into extinction, altering erosive processes, and shattering ecosystems on a global scale. Some individuals possessed biochemistries able to resist the infection. They survived and proliferated, and all *Zostera* seen today are their descendents. Similarly, the insecticide DDT prompted the emergence of insects that were not only resistant to its effects, but in several cases actually became addicted to the substance. These two instances involved significant biochemical reorganizations, and we mention them here because they are important examples of species response to massive selection pressures; and also because they illustrate evolutionary changes that will not be preserved in the fossil record (organisms may have undergone considerable modification of their soft parts and biochemistry without altering their skeletons).

The formation of a new taxonomic group may require no more than an alteration of a single gene. There are thousands of genes on a typical chromosome and, if the changed gene is at the base of a crucial developmental pathway, a pyramid effect may resound through the entire organism and change it in a variety of unanticipated ways. David Raup of Chicago's Field Museum of Natural History has shown that the basic forms of mollusk shells—ranging from clams to snails, scaphopods, and nautiloids—can be generated by varying only three simple gradients of growth. Using a computer program, he can construct a model of a snail shell on a television screen and allow us to see through it in all three dimensions. Then, starting with a young snail, and modifying two of the three generating forces, he can change the snail's shell into that of a common clam. Commenting on this development, Stephen Jay Gould wrote:

> . . . and believe it or not, a peculiar genus of modern snails does carry a bivalve shell so like a conventional clam's that I gasped when I saw a snail's head poking out between the valves in a striking close-up movie.

This is not to say that evolution depends upon the emergence of "hopeful monsters" (after all, we do not see many of them running around). David Raup's model is simply an illustration of how easily new taxa can be constructed from old blueprints. Most snails would die if their shells were changed suddenly into valves. The new shape would carry the old nervous, digestive, and circulatory systems right along with it. The stomach, for example, might end up twisted and in the wrong place, setting so many delicate organs awry that the creature could not survive. We can, however, imagine a rare and simple species built in such a way that its organ systems remain functional in spite of the new shell form. We might say that it has the necessary equipment arranged in just the right configuration to leave a certain developmental pathway open (a pathway that is closed to all other snails). Should individuals with bivalved shells arise, they would become monsters with hope. Which brings us to the question of what species may or may not build from the equipment at their disposal.

Crabs, like insects, spiders, and other arthropods, have managed to breach terrestrial barriers. Yet, while insects, and arachnids have penetrated even into the deserts of our world, crabs and hermit crabs will never be found very far from water. Their colonization of the land seems to be limited by what literally amounts to poor waterproofing. Insects, spiders, and scorpions possess a waxy layer in their exoskeletons, which crustacea seem unable to develop. Perhaps they simply lack the basic equipment from which wax-secreting glands can be derived, or maybe developmental constraints prevent them from arising because they disrupt the operation of more important systems and decrease the chances of larval and adult survival.

The first thing one notices about the robber crab *Birgo latro* is its size. This animal, a Pacific hermit crab that has given up the habit of carrying a mollusk shell around on its back, spends almost all of its time on land. It is reputed to climb coconut palms and eat the nuts. (Actually, *B. latro* is a rather poor climber, quite incapable of opening coconuts, and it seems to climb trees only to escape house cats and other predators; this tactic is one of doubtful merit, however, because the crabs often have great difficulty getting down again. Once on the ground, they live up to their name, which they have earned by walking away with anything they can grab. One researcher mentions sandals, cooking tins, knives, forks, and a wristwatch.) Robber crabs are among the largest of all crabs. In fact, largeness seems to be a feature shared by crabs living in terrestrial environments (although none become so large that they can not move about on land). One might explain this fact by pointing to the strong relationship between large size, a decrease in relative surface area, and lower rates of desiccation to counterbalance poor waterproofing. This can be shown experimentally by measuring the hour-by-hour evaporation of water from crabs of known surface areas and volumes. Another observer, however, might look at land crabs and conclude that large size makes them heavier and thus harder for birds and cats to carry off. A third might argue that large size leads to thicker shells and larger claws (the better to defend themselves against kids with sticks). And all three explanations are probably correct.

Too often, we are tempted to seek only one explanation for a given result; but nature does not seem to work that way. We can expect selection to operate most effectively when a direction offers multiple advantages and, as such, becomes self-reinforcing. The webs of skin between the limbs of flying Australian possums, squirrels, and bats serve not only for flight, but also radiate excess body heat. Selection preserves optimal solutions to common problems and, if a single adaptation can solve more than one problem, it will be fostered—*very quickly*. Such solutions are likely to turn up unexpectedly in totally unrelated species.

Hexagons appear repeatedly in objects as diverse as heterocyclic organic molecules, virus particles, the supporting structures of plants, the facets of an insect's eye, the cells of a honeycomb, and the interlocking plates in the armor of turtles, certain extinct fishes, and dinosaurs. The shape has become universal because, unlike circles, hexagons can be packed shoulder-to-shoulder to fill space completely without leaving wasteful holes between them. Moreover, they maximize the area within their confines, permitting each facet of an insect's eye to gather the greatest amount of light, or a stalk to transport the greatest volume of water to its leaves with a minimum of building materials (protein). They are structurally stable, resistant to external pressure, and not easily broken (especially when arranged in arrays). We should not be surprised if we discover hexagons wherever life has evolved.

Darwinian selection is mathematically destined to require that there be winners and losers (some losers, even, with hexagons). Sedimentary rocks are strewn with the corpses of winners that appeared in rapid bursts, persisted unchanged over millions of years, and then abruptly became losers—vanishing in a geological nanosecond.

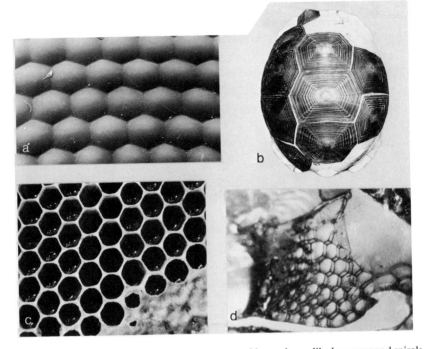

Because they provide optimal solutions to common problems, shapes like hexagons and spirals appear repeatedly in nature, sometimes in combination (as in the case of pine cones). Hexagons, shown here, are resistant to breakage, especially when arranged in arrays. They fill space completely without leaving wasteful holes between them. The hexagon is found in such diverse places as the facets of an insect's eye (*a*), the interlocking plates of a tortoise's shell (*b*), cells of a honeycomb (*c*), and the vascular structures of a 40-million-year-old plant preserved in Dominican amber (*d*). *Photos by C. R. Pellegrino.*

Approximately 160 million years ago, fossil-forming sediments began to trap the bones of animals belonging to the genus *Archaeopteryx*. According to traditional models, the bones belong to the forerunners of modern birds; but *Archaeopteryx* faded from the fossil record 140 million years ago, leaving behind no line of descent that can be traced from *Archaeopteryx* to a hummingbird or a condor. Nor can we follow the long heritage of *Archaeopteryx* through a series of transitional fossils (showing an accumulation of small changes) to a parting of branches at some reptilian/avian junction. Yet dinosaurs and *Archaeopteryx* were clearly related. The paradox is blamed (at times for no clear reason other than force of habit) on gaps in the fossil record. Gould views these gaps as an artifact of the jerky mode of speciation; in other words, they may be more real than apparent.

While the fossil record is indeed imperfect, there are, emerging from some quarters, compelling arguments that closer attention should be paid to imperfections of our questions about the record.

11
Ebb Tide

Augustus' (*Roman Emperor: 31 B.C. to A.D. 14*) *own country houses were modest enough and less remarkable for their statuary and pictures than for their landscape gardening and the rarities on display: for example, at Capreae he had collected the huge skeletons of extinct sea and land monsters popularly known as "Giants' Bones."*

Gaius Suetonius

Fifty million years lay under my feet, fifty million years of bellowing monsters moving in a green world now gone so utterly that its very light was traveling on the far edge of space. The chemicals of all that vanished age lay about me in the ground. The iron did not remember the blood it had once moved within, the phosphorus had forgot the savage brain. . . . I had lifted up a fistful of that ground. I held it while a wild flight of warblers hurtled over me into the oncoming dark. There went phosphorus, there went iron, there went carbon, there beat the calcium in those hurrying wings. Alone on a dead planet I watched that incredible miracle speeding past. It ran by some true compass over field and waste land. It cried its individual ecstasies into the air until the gullies rang. It swerved like a single body, it knew itself, and lonely, it bunched close in the racing darkness, its individual entities feeling about them in the rising night. And so, crying out to each other their identity, they passed away and out of my view.

Loren Eiseley

The crab maneuvered with swift precision under the incessant glimmer of a liquid sky. Fluid wind came creeping over the bottom, bringing with it breath, and nourishment, and tidings of distant happenings to the myriad animals dwelling in tubes, burrows, underground chambers, and passageways that honeycombed the broad sandy plains. A shrimp, flailing its antennae in the current, sensed something new in the air, summoned swimmerettes into motion, and took the sky. Chemosensors primed and working, the shrimp proceeded—sniffing the gradient—skimming low over the snails that plodded steadily toward a common goal. The world became filled with frantic crisscrossing traffic, bursting everywhere, forcing the shrimp down to the sea floor, just short of its reward. A roiling mass swirled about the carcass of a large animal. Everywhere the sky boiled with aggressive hordes of scavenging creatures that spun wildly and raced and glinted in the day-lit waters.

The shrimp rose and joined the swarm, oblivious to the huge shape that circled quietly, then descended like an anvil into the accumulation. A shark had seized the carcass, shaking its head furiously from side to side, gaping and swallowing, flushing its gills to rid itself of shrimp and amphipods as it tore off a mouthful of food and then departed quickly and silently into the blueness. The momentarily dispersed aggregation imploded on the body of the dead animal, and on those of its own number killed or maimed in the attack.

A coiled cephalopod, attracted by the mounting commotion, had singled out and now pursued a solitary crab. The unfortunate animal followed a zigzag line of hasty retreat, its claws outstretched in a futile display of aggression. The ammonite advanced ever so slowly, hovering, toying with its prey and waiting patiently for the tiring crab to seek shelter in the soft bottom. But the crab was saved. Titanic jaws closed down on the ammonite's shell, piercing it as though merely an egg. A giant reptile glided casually over the sea floor, stirring up puffs of churning sediment in its wake. Still grinding down the remains of the ammonite, the mosasaur began to seek out new food. It moved off and became a distant, lingering shadow—vast, crocodile-like, grotesque, and strange. . . .

Seventy million years passed. The oceans receded, advanced, and receded again. Forests swept over the new land, grew up, and remained there. Rivers and streams became scratches in the Earth's surface, exposing an ancient world that lay hidden beneath the fertile Marlborough plains of New Jersey. The mosasaur's teeth and fragmented bones now remain locked and preserved in the sea-floor

Mosasaurus maximus Cope, a giant crocodile-like lizard, patrolled New Jersey waters nearly 70 million years ago. Although *Mosasaurus* reached a length of 12 meters (approximately 40 feet), most reptiles (including the dinosaurs) of this period were considerably smaller. Many, in fact, were smaller than today's chickens. Shown here is the profile of a completely restored fossil skull on exhibit at the New Jersey State Museum in Trenton. *Photo by C. R. Pellegrino. Reprinted with permission from G. R. Case's A Pictorial Guide to Fossils (Van Nostrand Reinhold, 1982).*

sediments. The clay-like marls, for which the district is named, contain the chambered segments of ammonites—once dominant, now extinct.

About 65 to 90 million years ago, the great world-wide change began; it was characterized most prominently by the eclipse of reptiles and the rise to dominance of birds and mammals. The late Cretaceous extinctions ran parallel on land and sea, covering the entire phyletic spectrum. From Arctic to Antarctic, fully one-quarter of all known animal families, and an uncountable number of plants, vanished from the fossil record in the short span of a few million years. The Cretaceous-Tertiary boundary, about 65 million years ago, marks one of Earth history's most striking episodes of biological revolution and mass extinction. Not even the insects, often regarded as an ancient and invariable class of animals, emerged unscathed. The list of casualties includes several varieties of clams and almost all surviving brachiopods, which looked like clams. Many nautiloid species died out, as did their cousins the ammonites. They were accompanied by oceanic plankton, certain fishes, and dinosaurs.

Since the Cretaceous extinction included the largest—and possibly the most fascinating—animals ever to roam the continents, it has become the focus of much inquiry. The search for causes has been likened to a scientific parlor game, and the plethora of speculations advanced so far would fill a Los Angeles Telephone Directory. Most of these proposals falter because they are applied exclusively to the dinosaurs, typically to complications arising from their large size—food supply, mobility, coordination, even sexual problems—in spite of the fact that many, if not most, dinosaurs were smaller than house cats. Every five years or so, someone proposes in all seriousness that the dinosaurs had poor taste buds and were thus unable to detect the bitter, poisonous alkaloids in new species of flowering plants. One is tempted to ask how giant sea-going reptiles and little clams and single-celled, amoebalike animals went extinct eating the same plants.

In recent years, interest has centered on catastrophic models for extinction, particularly those attributed to extraterrestrial causes, for example a nearby supernova or, as some would have it, diseases from outer space, which brings us back to asteroids.

Interest in these bodies has been kindled by a team headed by Nobel Laureate Luis Alvarez and his geologist son, Walter, at Berkeley, California. Searching for a standard element, against which the relative deposition rates of sediments could be scaled, the Alvarez research group had hoped to use iridium. Iridium, like other heavy, unreactive metals in the platinum group (which also includes osmium and rhodium), is very rare in rocks of the Earth's crust and upper mantle. What little iridium fell onto the Earth's surface during its infancy is believed to have sunk toward the core. But iridium is one to ten thousand times more abundant in unmelted, undifferentiated stony meteorites. Working from the hypothesis that most iridium in the Earth's sediments comes from extraterrestrial sources, and that its arrival in meteorites and cosmic dust occurs as a fairly constant, world-wide rain, the Alvarez group reasoned that sediments high in iridium must have been exposed to this rain for a long time and thus would have formed slowly.

There was nothing wrong with the idea, in theory, but from the beginning everything seemed to be going wrong. The first measurements, made on 65-million-year-old deposits from the Umbrian Apennines of Italy, gave results that were far too high (30 times higher than average background concentrations in younger sedimentary

Cretaceous-Tertiary sediments at Petriccio, Italy, are shown in this photo by Walter Alvarez. Deposits 65 million years old bearing evidence for a terminal Cretaceous asteroid impact are being sampled by graduate students Stephen Marshak and William Leith from a recess below the overhanging limestone. The sedimentary layer immediately below the recess is from the Cretaceous period. Above it, in the overhang, are younger sediments of the Tertiary period. *Courtesy of Walter Alvarez.*

layers immediately above and in older layers immediately below) to account for a steady influx of iridium. Samples taken near Copenhagen, Denmark, proved disconcerting at best (160 times higher than average). A merely clever researcher might have dismissed these results immediately as absurd or, in his wish to be right—just this once—forced the data, like mismatched pieces of a puzzle, to fit the original hypothesis. (A willingness to have one's skyscrapers torn down, rather than *machismo,* is often the route to exotic discovery.)

Both samples came from thin clays deposited at the Cretaceous-Tertiary boundary, which was coincident with the great extinction. And herein lies a connection that has drawn considerable attention. The Berkeley investigators have proposed that vast quantities of iridium arrived instantaneously at the very top of the Cretaceous in the form of a Manhattan Island-sized asteroid. Such an object would have impacted on the Earth's surface at approximately 32 kilometers

(20 miles) per second, possessing energy equivalent to more than 100 times its weight in nitroglycerine and, the Alvarezes calculate, belching more dust into the air than several thousand Mount St. Helens. Their model then calls for a darkening of our entire planet, leading to a masking of photosynthesis and the immediate collapse, from the bottom up, of an orderly global ecology.

The geochemical clues pointing to an extraterrestrial origin of heavy metals in Cretaceous sediments has begun to pile up. Iridium and platinum concentrations 20 times higher than normal background levels have been found in rock strata from New Zealand and the central North Pacific. The extraterrestrial source could not have been a nearby supernova, for an exploding star would have deposited high concentrations of plutonium 244, aluminum 26, and other unusual isotopes alongside the iridium. None of these has been found.

While there can be little doubt that the Alvarezes have indeed uncovered evidence for an asteroid impact at the close of the Cretaceous, we are likely to discover, when the dust settles, that the event is being given too much credit (or blame) for the plight of dinosaurs and their contemporaries. The "ten years of darkness" scenario stands on unsteady ground and may well be sent scattering in pieces, especially if, as appears to be the case, the asteroid impacted on water. (After all, it is difficult for nature to hide a crater some 100 miles across, given only 65 million years to do so.) The current literature is filled with puzzlement over the five-fold disagreement between the Italian and Danish samples and, interestingly enough, very few people seem to be asking where the crater might be. If the anomalous iridium levels are viewed as a concentration gradient leading to the source, then they point almost like a finger toward the North Sea, and there, nearly 325 kilometers (200 miles) east of Dundee, Scotland, lies another anomaly: a 250 meter (820 foot) deep depression on the sea floor known as the Devil's Hole. The "hole" forms an almost perfect circle, measuring over 80 kilometers (50 miles) in diameter.

"If it did strike the Earth, it would be as if the Devil had struck with an enormous hammer," wrote Larry Niven and Jerry Pournelle in *Lucifer's Hammer*. It would seem that the Devil's Hole could not have been more appropriately named.

In conflict with the Alvarez scenario, much of the energy from such a strike would have been transferred immediately to the surrounding air and water (we can assume that the North Sea, which is very stable geologically, was a fairly isolated body of water, as it is today, 65 million years ago), injecting mountain ranges of steam high into the atmosphere. Granted, it would have rained like the Devil in the Northern Hemisphere, but the rains would also have carried most of the churned-up dust to the ground with them, and only stratospheric particles would have lingered for any length of time. A slight, yet short-lived cooling of temperatures—yes. A darkening of the entire planet —extremely doubtful.

The direct effects can be regarded as a fairly local event, limited chiefly to Europe and what was a then-considerably-narrower Atlantic Ocean. Certainly it was bad news for anybody underneath, and we don't envy any reptilian observer on the western shores of Denmark who might have watched the violent retreat of the sea and beheld a distant shadow that rose in frightful majesty, pushing even the clouds before it. But as far as the Earth is concerned, in both geological and biological terms, the impact of an average-sized asteroid should amount to little more than a celestial hiccup. (However, the two proposed impact features that form the Hudson Bay on the Canadian Shield, dating back to at least 3.9 billion years ago, may qualify as whooping cough.)

This by no means diminishes the greatness of the Alvarez's discovery. In fact, we are very eager to see analyses of core samples from the Devil's Hole and its surroundings.

As to the mass extinction problem, it appears doubtful that any one factor can, by itself, be credited. We are perhaps viewing a situation analogous to the 1979 "plague" of yellow-faced wasps on Long Island, New York, wherein all or most of the survival characteristics for the species (temperature, food supply, moisture, etc.) seemed to line up very favorably, resulting in a population surge.

The end of the Cretaceous might have seen something like this acting in reverse. Probably, climate will prove to be the main culprit: not so much a cooling off as a general decline of equability (more on this later). Toss in an Apollo object (any member of the largest family of Earth-crossing asteroids), one or two reversals of the Earth's magnetic poles (which are known to occur approximately every 700,000 years), and a slow but profound draining of the continental shelves, then sprinkle lightly with radioactive elements—the wreckage of a nearby star, perhaps—and it can become pretty tough going if you happen to be a dinosaur, or even an insect, for that matter. Stephen Jay Gould writes:

> I also agree that an extraterrestrial event could only have been a contributing factor to the great extinction. . . . But I do think that the astronomical catastrophe may have been more than just a minor *coup de grâce.* After all, extinctions far less extensive than the Cretaceous event have punctuated the history of life many times during the past 600 million years. Perhaps they never have really great impact unless the general deterioration of conditions that serves as their major cause is greatly amplified in effect by some major extraterrestrial event. Correspondingly, if the extraterrestrial event occurs during "good" biological times, maybe nothing much happens at all.

The current age of inquiry has shown that the Earth's surface is peppered with eroded, often "fossilized" remnants of impact features. *Landsat* imagery has confirmed the presence of several multikilometer scars, as for example the El'gygytgyn crater in northeastern Siberia, which dates back to as recently as 700,000 years ago and, in the fury of its birth, is believed to have jetted pieces of the surrounding countryside into the vacuum of near space, where they scattered, molten, and rained down as far away as Indochina and Australia (our human forbears were around to witness this event).

Massive cratering events are rare today, their frequency having declined quickly about 3.7 to 3.9 billion years ago, following a heavy bombardment of the planets and their satellites by infalling bodies. Presumably, this was the final stage in the sweeping up of debris left over from the primordial dust cloud (a process which, according to analyses of rock samples from Greenland and the *Apollo* landing sites, culminated in the formation of the Earth's crust some 4.45 billion years ago). Even during this period of intense bombardment, preliving chemical evolution must have commenced in our seas. Arriving asteroids would only have stirred the mixture of water and silt and organic compounds, while at the same time injecting new energy into the system, so that, by 4.0 billion years ago (but probably many millions of years earlier), our most remote ancestors would have ap-

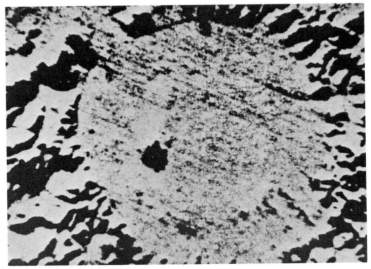

Tectites are shock-melted glass, differing considerably from natural volcanic glass. The tear-drop shapes and surface markings on these samples from Sri Lanka (the larger is 50 mm long) are the result of atmospheric ablation. Potassium-argon isotope dating and fission-track analysis (the amount of damage done to crystals by the decay of radioactive elements incorporated in the rocks) have yielded an approximate age of 700,000 years, which corresponds closely with the estimated age of the El'gygytgyn Crater in northeastern Siberia. *Photos by C. R. Pellegrino.*

peared: microscopic bags of polymer, possibly lacking DNA, but nevertheless capable of using certain molecules (for example, the flattened, ring-like porphyrins) for the storage and release of energy. During the 500 million years that followed, as asteroids continued to hammer at the Earth, not only did actual living cells evolve, but they also managed to establish complex ecosystems. Some used energy from the sun to process carbon from the environment, while others devoured their neighbors, and still others, looking like strings of beads, took the crucial evolutionary step to multicellularity.

The thought that excites the imagination, that should make the skin on the back of your head prickle, is that these creatures—the things that became us—emerged during the period of heaviest bombardment

---

The distribution of shock-melted pearls of glass, dating to about 700,000 years ago and scattered throughout Australia and Asia, reveals an axis pointing toward El'gygytgyn Crater in northeastern Siberia (*top*). The crater (*bottom*) measures 18 kilometers (11 miles) across, and may be the largest Quaternary impact scar on Earth. *Landsat photo courtesy of NASA's Lunar and Planetary Institute.*

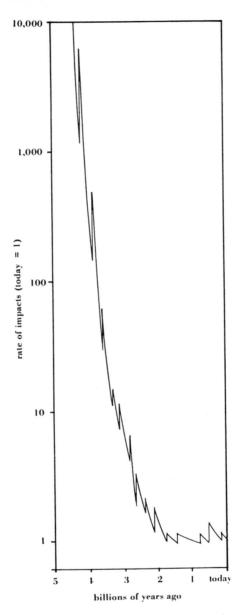

The Earth's cratering history has been reconstructed from counts of craters in different provinces on the moon whose ages are known from rock samples. The record suggests intense bombardment during our world's first billion years. Spikes in the declining curve mark periods of unusually intense bombardment. The spikes result from new material entering the solar system and/or from the shattering of large bodies outside the orbit of Mars.

of our planet's crust, almost literally as it was formed from a collapsing ball of gas and dust in space. And here we witness another extinction, of sorts: the fate of those little bags of polymer and energy-storing molecules. Although extinction appears to be the destiny of most species (usually explained as a failure to adapt rapidly enough to changing conditions), those energy-capturing bags might not have disappeared altogether. The oxidative energy that drives our cells is provided by microscopic engines called mitochondria. To our amazement, the whole concept of the "Stranger Within" has shifted from symbol and myth to a dawning realization that these and other organelles are not truly ours. Mitochondria carry their own stores of DNA and RNA, quite different from the DNA and RNA found in our cell nuclei. The inner membrane of a mitochondrian is distinct from the one lining the cell in which it drifts and more closely resembles a bacterial membrane. Their ribosomes are also different, belonging to separate creatures that replicate privately and in apparent independence of the cell. No nucleated cells in our bodies are without mitochondria. They infiltrate both sperm and egg, riding down with them to the first diploid cell of the newborn and dispersing their progeny through cleavage into succeeding generations of *Homo sapiens.*

There may be other aliens embedded in our cytoplasm: Cilia, flagella, and centrioles (barrel-shaped organelles from which the propulsive structures of cilia and flagella arise) are believed by some cell biologists to be self-reproducing organisms that formed symbiotic linkages with our forbears.

Photosynthetic engines, equipped with their own DNA, RNA, and ribosomes, apparently joined in partnership with primitive cells and became the chloroplasts of green plants. It begins to look as if chloroplasts and mitochondria, or something very much like them, were among the earliest recognizable life forms to appear on Earth. Think upon it the next time you hold a leaf in the palm of your hand.

Note: For an update on asteroid impacts and terrestrial evolution, readers are referred to the Winter 1982 issue of *Paleobiology* and the 21 May, 1982 issue of *Science.*

12
Death Watch

I would rather look at the entrails of chickens than try to predict solar activity.

Robert Frosch

A good friend of mine follows the stars,
Venus and Mars are alright tonight. *

Paul McCartney

Amber, a hardened resin exuded by plants occupying scattered positions within the botanical system, is found almost all over the world. Deposits of the "organic gem" have been laid down by the lives and deaths of forests ranging from Mississipian and Pennsylvanian times (approximately 290 to 347 million years ago) right up to the present, where it occurs in the form of its raw material, the fresh-flowing sap of trees.

Pieces of amber often contain fragments of fossil vegetation, mingled occasionally with feathers, mammalian hairs, and, most importantly, ancient and remarkably well-preserved insect bodies.

Our current knowledge places the emergence of insects approximately 400 million years ago. They would thus have originated as contemporaries of the first green plants to populate the land. No traces of these earliest insects have ever been positively identified, but they are believed to have evolved from certain many-legged marine animals.

The first insects to leave a permanent record of themselves in rocks flourished almost 100 million years later in the lush, gloomy forests of the Mississippian and Pennsylvanian periods (also referred to, together, as the Carboniferous), whose vegetation, alien in appearance and flowerless, eventually formed our fossil coal beds. One of the most impressive Coal Age insects was the giant dragonfly, *Meganeura monyi,* with a wingspan of over 90 centimeters (approximately 3 feet). Most insects of the Pennsylvanian have long since altered their shapes, and the majority, including *M. monyi,* have met with extinction; but a few, like the mayfly, cockroach, and primitive wingless insects of the subclass Apterygota, have persisted almost unchanged into the present.

Within the graves of Coal Age forests are also found the oldest known deposits of fossil resin, metamorphosed, shattered, and lacking insect remains. Ambers containing fossils are unearthed most commonly from strata deposited during the last 100 million years, a period whose rocks record one of Earth history's most recent and most striking biological revolutions: the Cretaceous-Tertiary transition from an age of reptiles to one of mammals.

What does amber tell us about this enigmatic chapter in the history of life?

A census of insects in Cretaceous amber from Canada (the amber has never been precisely dated, but is widely believed to have been formed at least 72 to 74 million years ago) and from the Atlantic Coastal Plain (where it formed approximately 100 million years ago) reveals that by middle to late Cretaceous time, though the living orders had already been established, many modern families did not yet exist and that none of the insects belonged to known genera or species. In contrast, practically all insects recovered from deposits in the Dominican highlands (ranging between 26 and 40 million years old) and the Baltic Coast (approximately 40 million years old) can be referred to existing families, about half to existing genera, and even a few to existing species. This is a very considerable change in the course of about 30 to 60 million years, and it is one that far exceeds changes

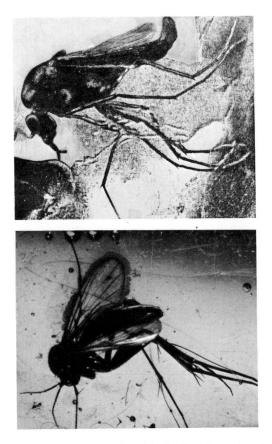

Two remarkably well preserved flies belonging to the family chironomidae (non-biting midges) are shown in amber. The fly (*on top*) was discovered in Sayrville, New Jersey, and flew among dinosaurs approximately 100 million years ago (magnification 30×, photo slightly retouched). The fly (*on bottom*) is a 40-million-year-old specimen from the amber forests of Northern Europe (magnification 30×). *Photos by C. R. Pellegrino.*

during the subsequent (Oligocene to present) 40 million years. Somewhat corresponding findings would appear to hold for portions of the plant kingdom and for such diverse animal groups as crabs and horses.

Although we have traditionally regarded insects as ancient and unchanging, the fossil record suggests that they emerged into the Tertiary looking very different from their Cretaceous forbears (the large central populations we see as fossils), as did the surviving branches of our own phylum.

The Cretaceous period was characterized by widespread shallow seas (much of the western and southern United States was then under water) and by a correspondingly uniform climate, under which subtropical forests flourished in northern Alaska. During the closing stages of the Cretaceous, long before the arrival of the Alvarez's asteroid, the ammonites, dinosaurs, and other fauna had already begun to die out. By the end of the period, the porpoise-like ichthyosaurs and the stout-bodied, turtle-like plesiosaurs were gone. The mosasaurs were practically the only reptiles left in the oceans. Then they too died out.

The disappearance of mosasaurs at the Cretaceous-Tertiary boundary coincided with a gradual but profound drop in sea level, as recorded by world-wide breaks in marine sedimentation. The withdrawal of shallow seas from the area of the continents would have restricted the circulation of warm ocean water, leading to the buildup of ice at high latitudes and thus compounding the problem. The record does in fact show a slight cooling of the Earth's oceans about 70 million years ago, and deep sea cores taken east of New Zealand

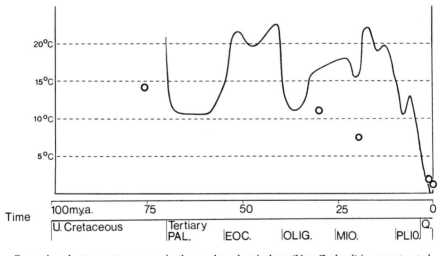

Cenozoic paleotemperature curve in the southern hemisphere (New Zealand) is reconstructed from changes in the diversity of planktonic foram species, oxygen isotope ratios, botanical fossils, and analyses of glacially derived ice-rafted sands in sub-Antarctic deep-sea cores. Dark circles represent secular cooling of deep ocean water, as indicated by oxygen isotope ratios and fossilized shells of deep-water foraminifera. The evidence points to climatic cooling across the Cretaceous-Tertiary boundary, with gradual recovery in late Paleocene time. *Compiled by C. R. Pellegrino.*

provide signs of glacially derived ice, at least in very high latitudes, as early as 55 million years ago; but the most dramatic climatic deterioration, the periods we call Ice Ages, did not commence until the beginning of the Oligocene epoch nearly 15 million years later. Paradoxically, the most pronounced variation in insects, and the plants to which many of them were associated, is seen from Cretaceous to Oligocene time rather than from Oligocene to the present.

Clearly, events preceding the Ice Ages, possibly the mere onset of climatic deterioration, exercised greater force than the Ice Ages themselves.

American Museum of Natural History paleobiologist Norman Newell has emphasized that the stability of physical settings characteristic of tropical organic reefs insulates the reef inhabitants from many of the stresses to which communities in more seasonal climates, for example the present-day New Jersey marshes, are exposed. Where environmental settings are stable, as in very deep water, a tropical reef, or under the canopy of a mangrove forest, interrelationships between competing species become the primary adaptive problem. As a rule, such places are inhabited by many different species, and these may form startlingly complex associations. The world comes alive with tensions, alarms, and homing beacons. Symbiotic linkages between ancestrally unrelated organisms abound: the algae that dwell inside coral polyps, the damsel fish that shelters among the lethal tentacles of certain anemones, and Lewis Thomas's celebrated medusa and the snail, among others.

Stable or equable climates need not be warm to affect the diversity of life. During his voyage around the world, Charles Darwin was impressed with the subtropical aspect of forests ranging close to the margin of South Polar climate in Chile and New Zealand. He found the forests of southern Chile dominated by tropical evergreens. These were carpeted with epiphytes and climbing vines, and they supported parrots as far south as the Strait of Magellan. He attributed these phenomena to the high equability of climate there.

Tropical evergreens are standing literally within meters of the Fox and the Franz Joseph glaciers, which descend almost to sea level near the west coast of South Island, New Zealand (they are currently melting back at rates approaching 15 meters annually). Both north and south of the glaciers, dark green foliage spreads an almost un-

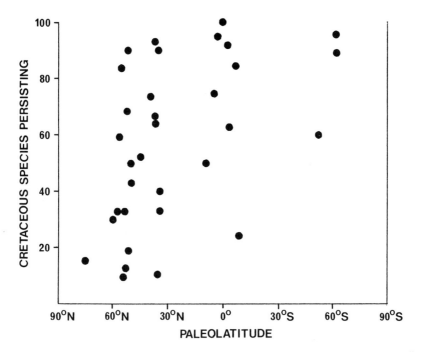

Survival of plant species across the Cretaceous-Tertiary boundary reveals a record of generally high floral survival from high-southern to mid-northern latitudes (Paleolatitudes represent positions of fossil sites corrected for continental drift). Cretaceous climate was characterized by a generally higher average Earth temperature and a lower gradient of temperatures from equator to pole (due largely to the absence of polar ice caps). A greater number of northern hemisphere species are represented here because the majority of stratigraphical sections containing both the last dinosaurs and fossil plants contemporary with them are found in western North America. *Compiled by L. J. Hickey, 1981.*

broken blanket over the land. The surrounding forest is populated by broad-leaved evergreens, tangles of epiphytes and lianas, an occasional palm, and tree ferns reaching 7 meters (approximately 23 feet) in height. Only 100 kilometers (62 miles) north of Franz Joseph glacier, dense groves of palm trees flourish.

Standing alone under a green canopy only 2 kilometers (less than 2 miles) from the terminal face of Fox glacier, in a world alive with birds and insects, a visitor from the northern hemisphere can not easily comprehend that he is located at a latitude corresponding to Portland, Maine, and to Rochester, New York—except, perhaps, for the slight chill in the air. The South Island forest provides strong contrast to

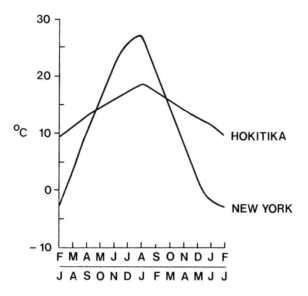

Differences in equability, or annual range of temperature, between Hokitika in New Zealand (latitude 43° south) and New York in the United States (latitude 41° north) are shown in this compilation from NOAA and DSIR records from 1975 through 1980. Modern plants most nearly related to those of the Mesozoic thrive in regions characterized by high equability. The relative stability of temperatures would seem to account for the subtropical appearance of New Zealand's South Island forests. The months at the bottom of the graph designate New York (*above*) and New Zealand (*below*), with summer maximums superimposed. The reversal of months illustrates opposite seasons on the northern and southern hemispheres.

Long Island in New York, which has nearly the same average yearly temperature (12.1° C) as Hokitika in New Zealand (14.0° C), but experiences much broader seasonal variations. For example, Shinnecock Bay, which is on Long Island, is almost "bathwater-warm" in the summer, and every year it becomes populated by tropical fish carried north by the Gulf Stream; yet there are winters within recent memory during which college students have driven cars across it. Trees fringing the bay include coniferous (cone-bearing) shrubs, pines, spruce, cedars, as well as hardwood deciduous (leaf-shedding) trees. Broad-leaved evergreens are absent. The nearest groves of palm trees are in Florida, and the closest tree ferns are in Mexico. The difference between Long Island in New York and South Island in New Zealand arises from the significantly greater coverage of the northern hemisphere by large land masses. Less of the sun's radiation becomes

A river of ice left over from the last glacial period is seen here in areal (*left*) and ground-level (*right*) views. New Zealand's Fox Glacier descends close to sea level, where it is within 2 kilometers (1.2 miles) of dense groves of tree ferns and an occasional palm. The subtropical aspect of the forests surrounding Fox Glacier is attributed to the high equability of climate there. *Photos by T. Pellegrino.*

trapped by water, and the circulation of warm ocean water is severely restricted by the exposure of vast continental boundaries, thus creating more extreme temperatures that vary with a seasonal and even a diurnal rhythm. Lower equability limits the northward extent of all but the most adaptable flora and fauna.

When you examine the fossil record, you find that some factor in the environment had enabled plants and animals to range very widely, to spread literally from pole to pole during the Mesozoic era (approximately 65 to 230 million years ago). Then, as the era drew to a close, some factor, or variety of factors, was forcing the extinction of many groups and greatly restricting the range of others. Yet, at the same time, certain groups (for example, birds, mammals, and several obscure insect families) began to radiate, diversify, and rise to dominance. One factor that seems to prevail throughout Jurassic and

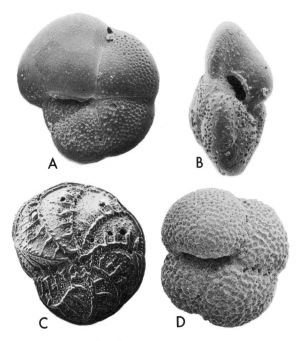

The story of the transition from a relatively unglaciated world to one characterized by on-again off-again Ice Ages is recorded in the shells of tiny plants and animals living in the oceans. As conditions change (if, for example, the oceans experience a geologically sudden episode of cooling), the types of shells accumulating on the ocean floor and the isotopic composition of their carbonate material will also change. A study of these changes shows a general decline of temperatures commencing approximately 65 to 70 million years ago and culminating in the present series of Ice Ages (with the most significant phase of Antarctic ice-cap growth beginning approximately 15 million years ago). Shown here are the skeletons of three species of amoeba-like foraminifera (each measuring approximately 100 μ across). *Globorotalia scitula* (*A* and *B*) is a deep-water species found almost all over the world. The species first appeared some 20 million years ago, and presently lives in waters heated to 10 to 20° C (temperate climate). *Notorotalia finlayi* (*C*), another deep-water species, is a characteristic temperate foram inhabiting deep water on New Zealand's continental shelf. *Neogloboquadrata pachyderma* (*D*) resides in near-surface water and is recognized as a southern hemisphere cold-water species. This species occurs as far south as Antarctica, but is also known from subtropical waters, where its shell cambers grow to the left. The warm-water variant is shown here. These specimens were recovered from sediments dating to approximately one million years ago. In life, they possessed long spines. These fell off once the animals settled to the bottom. *Photos courtesy of the New Zealand Physics and Engineering Laboratory, D.S.I.R.*

Cretaceous time (approximately 65 to 195 million years ago) is mild climate of pronounced equability. Presumably, life on Earth became highly adapted to global warmth that, as far as we can tell, lasted for nearly 130 million years.

The foraminifera are an order of tiny unicellular animals. Many species live in the surface water of the ocean and are distributed worldwide. They are related to the common amoeba, but possess elaborate, basket-like shells. These shells accumulate on the sea floor, sometimes forming great beds of limestone (such as the quarries fringing the Nile River, from which blocks were cut to build the pyramids). As temperature and other conditions change, the diversity of foram species in sea-floor sediments and the isotopic composition of oxygen in their calcium carbonate skeletons also change. The study of fossil foram shells in deep-sea cores tells a story of decreasing marine temperatures accompanied by rapid cycles of atmospheric heating and cooling near the end of the Cretaceous.

That static temperatures became manifest in middle and higher latitudes at the Cretaceous-Tertiary boundary is supported by University of California paleobotanist Daniel Axelrod's census of succeeding Paleocene flora (57 to 65 million years old) from Wyoming, western Canada, and Greenland. He notes in particular a transition from fossil leaves with smooth margins to species with serrated margins typified by deciduous hardwoods, implying a shift toward more distinct winters and summers. Resin-secreting "gum trees" belonging to the family araucariaceae ranged widely over the globe during Mesozoic time, but they retreated from the northern hemisphere (where they had laid down the Canadian and North American amber deposits) soon after the close of the Cretaceous. They (or close relatives) advanced briefly into the Dominican Republic and northern Europe during a period of Eocene-Oligocene warming (approximately 40 million years ago), and now persist chiefly in the southern hemisphere. They are found in areas of high equability, notably in the Philippines (a tropical region) and New Zealand (a temperate region).

Only a small decline in annual temperature may lead to a marked decline of equability. Isotopic analyses of fossil forams suggest that average temperatures of the sea surface at middle and high latitudes decreased about 5° C (9° F) during the closing stages of the Cretaceous period. In Campanian time (approximately 76 million years ago) the termperature difference between equatorial and polar seas has been estimated as 11° C (20° F), compared with about 15° C (27° F) during the Maastrichtian stage (approximately 70 million years ago, during which time Marlborough, New Jersey, still lay under water). Air temperatures over the continents must have been considerably more extreme.

Exactly what this meant to dinosaurs can be judged partly from the temperature tolerances of surviving reptiles. In his work with living alligators, vertebrate paleontologist Edwin Colbert found that, because of their large ratio of volume to surface area, any rise in the body temperatures of adult alligators exposed to direct sunlight occurred very slowly, and the loss of body heat in the shade was also slow. By regulating their exposure to the sun, alligators can maintain an optimal body temperature with minimal output of energy simply by basking in the sun's rays and then moving into water for a few hours. Colbert suggests that large dinosaurs behaved in a similar fashion, using the shade of trees during the daytime or alternating between sunny areas and relatively cooler rivers, lakes, and low-lying marshlands. If the search for food (or the avoidance of being searched for as food) required that an alligator-like dinosaur spend several hours in the hot sun, no great rise in body temperature would be experienced. The animal thus conserved freedom of movement, and such a relationship would have been aided by equable climates that oscillated only slightly above and below the reptile's mean body temperature. Under these conditions, large dinosaurs might have gained some of the advantages provided by homiothermy (the maintenance of a specific body temperature by warm-blooded vertebrates, which is about 37° C in humans) even without an internal-termperature regulatory system of their own. (There has been speculation, based upon a growing body of evidence, including the discovery of "hairy dinosaurs," that some Mesozoic reptiles were warm-blooded. The verdict is not yet in, but we will probably learn that temperature regulation in dinosaurs ranged from true homiothermy down to the mode exhibited by today's alligators. After all, even some sharks are warm-blooded.)

The fossil remains of small dinosaurs reveal no clues that they had adopted burrowing habits, like lizards, snakes, turtles, and some mammals did, or that they hibernated like alligators and other modern reptiles. Such habits would have enabled them to escape the effects of winter extremes but, if small dinosaurs did not burrow or hibernate, they would have been more sensitive to temperature changes than were their giant cousins. They were therefore more dependent on equable climate than were the larger dinosaurs, turtles, lizards, and snakes that stirred among them and eventually outlived them (if only by a short time, in the case of large dinosaurs, whose most recent Paleocene fossils date back to about 60 million years ago).

Although we can observe the results of high or low equability by a simple comparison of Long Island, New York, with South Island, New Zealand, we do not yet have a clear understanding of how variable temperatures inhibit the survival of certain plant and animal groups. Lethal extremes, such as freezing during the winter, need never be reached to prevent coconut palms and alligators from establishing themselves in North Carolina. Experiments suggest that cold-blooded vertebrates exposed to temperatures higher than their adapted norm will suffer a loading effect, sometimes necessitating a rapid or steady release of energy. Cold temperatures act in the opposite direction, inducing an unloading or inhibitory effect on metabolic function. They may, in a manner of speaking, encounter an "energy crisis," which reduces the effectiveness of normal functions such as feeding, growth, resistance to disease, and successful reproduction.

We don't have to resort to pictures of advancing waves of ice to explain the disappearance of dinosaurs. Increasing summer extremes, operant across middle and higher latitudes, could have worked in unison with cooler winters to bring about their demise. If ice alone were required to incite a biological revolution, then widespread extinctions would not have been seen until 40 to 55 million years ago, and dinosaurs would now be rasping and hissing on the equator. Apparently, whatever was happening at higher latitudes also had a penetrating effect on the inner tropics.

The last billion years of our planet's history have been punctuated by five major Ice Ages: in the late Precambrian period, coincident with the emergence of trilobites and most of the known phyla (about 570 million years ago) the late Ordovician (approximately 435 million years ago); the Mississippian and Pennsylvanian periods, which saw on-again off-again glacial advances that intensified at the Permian-Triassic boundary (approximately 230 million years ago); a short-lived glacial period at the Triassic-Jurassic boundary (approximately 200 million years ago); and during the latter two-thirds of the Cenozoic Era (from approximatley 40 million years ago to the present). Ice sheets at the Earth's poles stand as ominous reminders that we are still in the grip of the latest Ice Age.

Each episode of glaciation appears to have been accompanied by (or, more correctly, preceded by) a biological revolution. Our most detailed records come from relatively recent strata (of course!); and some fossils exhibit striking correlations of diversity and structure with periods of known climatic deterioration. In this sense, the ammonites seem to be a veritable barometer, their numbers waxing and waning with periods of differing equability. More than half of the ammonite species died out as the Mississippian glaciations commenced, but their diversity gradually increased through Pennsylvanian time. The group suffered near extinction during the late Permian and late Triassic ice advances, reestablished itself in unprecedented numbers during the Jurassic period, dwindled slightly at the Jurassic-Cretaceous boundary, and then diversified again before finally expiring during the late Cretaceous. We wish to argue that the ammonites had more limited tolerance for temperature fluctuations than their nautiloid cousins, and that their temporary decline at the Jurassic-Cretaceous boundary—a time that corresponds with moderate changes in other phyla and whose 141-million-year-old rocks betray no signs of frost—indicates a period of mild climatic deterioration.

We may owe our existence to a geologically sudden and widespread change, or to a series of changes, that extinguished most large reptiles and yet allowed our mammalian ancestors to tread upon the Earth and dominate it. If not for the cold, a flock of pterosaurs might now be surveying New Jersey from on high and there would be no telescopes, music, or questions.

But what caused such changes in the first place? How did a planet that supported forests in northern Alaska and Greenland during one era manage to spread a 3 kilometer (2 mile) thick blanket of ice over North America in the next?

Ice tends to accumulate when large masses of land are at or near the poles. When we reconstruct the history of tectonic movements, we learn that, as the Permian drew to a close, South America, South Africa, Madagascar, India, Australia, Antarctica, and New Zealand

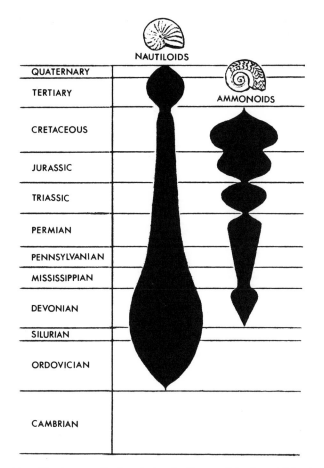

The ammonoids suffered near extinction during the Permeo-Triassic and Triassic-Jurassic ice advances, followed by a decline of numbers at the Jurassic-Cretaceous boundary and extinction during the closing stages of the Cretaceous period. The nautiloids, a related group, endured the Cretaceous-Tertiary extinctions and even increased their numbers during the Tertiary time (possibly owing to ecological replacement of the ammonoids). They have not fared as well through the climatic upheavals of the last 3 million years. *The chart is based on the work of George Gaylord Simpson and Norman Newell.*

were all brought into close contact near the South Pole and became the center of the supercontinent of Pangea. The continent developed an ice sheet that radiated from South Africa, expanding and shrinking and causing the sea to advance and retreat repeatedly. At the end of the Permian period, the ice cap grew to dimensions that have not been

The Laurentide ice sheet, seen in its maximum extent approximately 14,000 years ago.

matched since. Rivers of ice extended almost to North America's Coal Age marshes, which were located on the equator. In the seas, fully *one-half* of all animal families disappeared. The ammonites had a close call. The few surviving trilobites were not so lucky.

Then, as the Mesozoic Era began, Pangea broke up, the ice sheet melted, and shifting plates carried most of the pieces northward, until the land masses became concentrated in their present positions around the North Pole, leading to the accumulation of more ice.

On the Mid-Atlantic Ridge, where part of the system that fractured Pangea is pushing Europe and North America apart at a velocity of several centimeters per year, huge convective currents in the Earth's mantle are bringing hot rocks and basaltic lava up to the surface. At the submarine ridge, and also in places like the Galápagos Rift, the earth is releasing internal heat. The Mid-Atlantic Ridge is activley producing new sea floor and pushing it outward from the source. The crust has swollen there, cracking and permitting sea water to seep

The Vatnajökull ice sheet covers about 8,400 square kilometers (5,220 square miles) of Iceland's southeastern coast. This Landsat view, taken on September 22, 1973, shows that the ice field is presently in a state of retreat. *Courtesy of the U.S. Geological Survey.*

down and return with stolen heat. While the crust remains active and swollen, water is displaced onto the continental shelves. Conversely, as heat is radiated and the swelling subsides, sea level falls, exposing larger continental boundaries, restricting warm-water flow, and increasing the severity of inland winters. If continents happen to be jammed around either pole, extensive glaciation may result, causing the seas to withdraw even faster. At some stage, growth of the ice sheet should become self-sustaining, irreversible. Its margins eventually creep into surface sea water, freezing it. The Earth's albedo (the ratio of sunlight reflected to that received) changes. Water vapor pass-

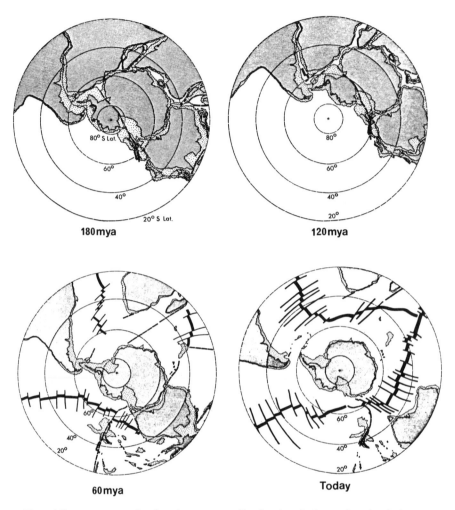

180 mya

120 mya

60 mya

Today

These 4 diagrams summarise changing patterns of land and sea in the southern hemisphere over the last 180 million years. The position of the South Pole is indicated by a star. Although the shapes of individual continents have changed considerably during geological time, modern shapes are used for ease of reference. *Adapted from G. Stevens, New Zealand Adrift (Reed, 1980).*

ing over the white blanket invariably falls as snow. Even if the continents scatter in pieces toward the opposite pole, they should leave behind them a frozen sea resembling the Arctic Ocean of today. Once established, ice caps can never go away—at least in theory.

This evidently does not happen. The late Permian ice cap disappeared completely, and forests spread across Antarctica even as it drifted to its present position at the South Pole, Sea floor spreading and the positions of continents alone are not the whole answer. Something else is superimposed over the Earth's own modifiers of climate (oceans, continents, and ice sheets). Some investigators believe that episodes of glacial growth and decay may have astronomical origins, including the wobbling motions of the Earth's rotation axis, which cause the amount of solar radiation falling on the equator during perihelion (the point at which our slightly elliptical orbit carries us nearest the sun) to vary with time. In the presence of ice sheets, the weak temperature fluctuations that result seem to be followed by large-scale oscillations.

Most of us have grown up believing that we orbit a stable star, but recent studies suggest that the sun has changed in size and brightness since you started reading this chapter. One way of observing these changes is to measure very precisely the Doppler shift of absorption lines in the sun's atmosphere and then compare them against a nearby

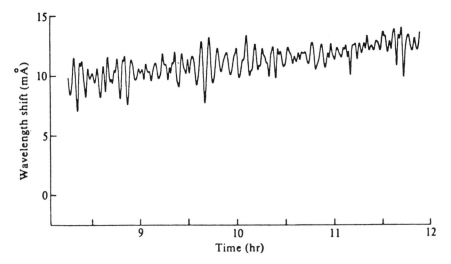

Wavelength shifts on the sun's disk suggest that the solar radius undergoes very small fluctuations, as though the sun were "breathing gently," with a period of about 5 minutes. The steady increase in wavelength seen here is an artifact of the observer's changing speed toward the sun (during the morning hours) due to the Earth's rotation. *Adapted from D. E. Blackwell.*

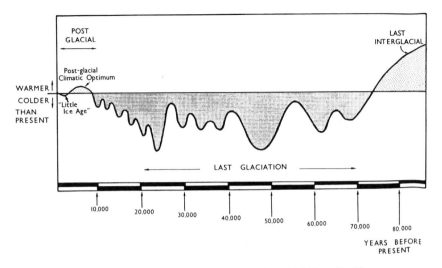

Oscillations within the last glaciation, which spanned from 75,000 to 10,000 years ago, are revealed by studies of tree rings, fossil pollen grains, and the skeletons of microscopic marine organisms. The postglacial climatic optimum, when average temperatures were 1 to 3° C (2 to 5°F) warmer than they are now, reached a peak between 3520 and 2020 B.C. The "Little Ice Age," ranging from about A.D. 1550 to 1800, produced the greatest extensions of ice on land and sea since the glaciations. *Reproduced from G. Stevens, New Zealand Adrift (Reed, 1980).*

absorption line in our own atmosphere. Because we are observing from the surface of a planet that is rotating on its axis as it orbits the sun, we want to subtract the difference between the motion of the observer and the observed. For this purpose, absorption lines in our own atmosphere serve as a point of reference from which the approach of the Earth-facing side of the sun (due to swelling), or its retreat (due to shrinking), can be deduced. Doppler shifts can be measured to such accuracy that it would be possible to discern the motion of a person walking toward us strictly by the *blueshift* of light reflected from him. We are therefore able to demonstrate that the solar radius fluctuates, as though the sun were "breathing gently," with a period of about five minutes.

Preliminary satellite observations suggest that solar luminosity can vary by about 0.10 percent over a 6-month period, and estimates of the sun's diameter, based upon the duration of totality for solar eclipses and timings of transits of the planet Mercury across the sun's face over the last 250 years, have yielded clues that the solar diameter

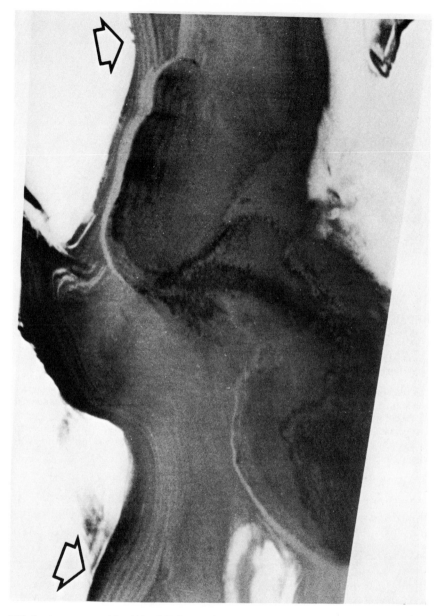

This frosty scene near Mars' North Pole was photographed by *Viking Orbiter 2* on October 26, 1976, during the northern summer when the carbon dioxide layer had evaporated to expose the water ice beneath. The area covered is approximately 60 by 30 kilometers (37 by 18 miles). The photograph shows distinct terraces or layers, suggesting that Mars has experienced cold periods alternating with warmer climate. Steps on the ice are about 50 meters (165 feet) thick, and their regularity suggests that cold periods recur every few hundred-thousand years or so. According to this interpretation, Mars is presently in the throes of an Ice Age. *Reprinted through the courtesy of National Aeronautics and Space Administration, California Institute of Technology, Jet Propulsion Laboratories.*

This winter scene on Mars' boulder-strewn Plain of Utopia was photographed by *Viking Lander 2* on May 18, 1979. The largest rocks shown here are nearly one meter across. The rocks and soil are coated with a light frost, which is thought to be a mixture of water ice and frozen carbon dioxide similar in composition to the material covering Mars' polar regions. *Reprinted through the courtesy of National Aeronautics and Space Administration, California Institute of Technology, Jet Propulsion Laboratories.*

may change by approximately 0.02 percent during 80-year cycles. If that does not seem to be dramatic, consider, if you will, what cycles may occur over thousands or millions of years. The surface of Mars provides circumstantial evidence. Like Earth, the planet is in the throes of an Ice Age. *Viking Orbiter* images showing the edges of the polar caps reveal distinct layers or terraces of water-ice (during the summer season, when the overlaying cover of carbon dioxide frost has boiled off). The terraces suggest that Mars has experienced warm periods alternating with colder climate, and their thickness indicates that warm periods recur every few hundred-thousand years or so.

The Martian landscape seems to tell a tale of ancient and rather extreme climatic fluctuations, characterized by increased atmospheric

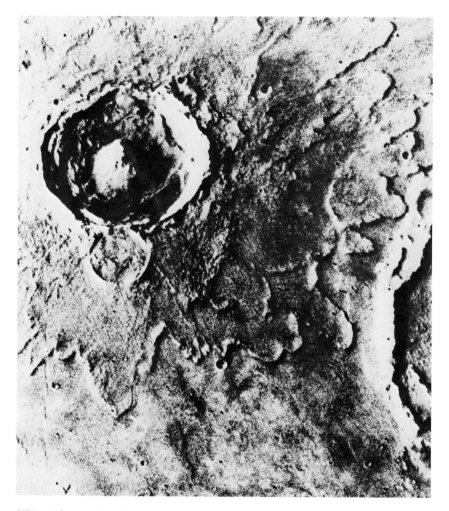

Viking 1 photographed the crater Yuty from a range of 1877 kilometers (1165 miles) on June 22, 1976. The crater measures 18 kilometers (11 miles) across. The lobate extensions suggest that a considerable amount of water lies frozen as permafrost in the Martian soil. According to astronomer Carl Sagan, it is hard to interpret these features as anything but liquified mud, flowing away from the crater following localized melting of permafrost upon impact. They cannot be lava flows because the meteorite that formed the crater was too small to melt large volumes of rock. *Reprinted through the courtesy of National Aeronautics and Space Administration, California Institute of Technology, Jet Propulsion Laboratories.*

pressure, extensive wind erosion, and at least one major episode of liquid water breaking out across the planet's surface. (Recent observations suggest that the near-equatorial Solis Lacus region of Mars, known as an "oasis" of water outgassing, may have a reservoir of very salty liquid water residing within one meter of the surface.) The last major erosional period, dating back at least several tens-of-millions of years, appears to have ended abruptly. Are climatic fluctuations on Mars synchronous with glacial advances and retreats on Earth? If they are (and we have not yet examined both planets closely enough to answer this question), then they may be tied to variations in the intensity of radiation from our sun.

Solar neutrinos provide a unique opportunity for probing fusion reactions occurring deep in the sun's core. Neutrinos are "ghostly" particles. Born in reactions involving the so-called "weak force" that governs the decay of atomic nuclei, their interactions with all other matter in the universe are weak—so weak that by the time you finish reading this sentence, trillions of them will have shot through your body without bumping into anything. In fact they can pass clear through the Earth. At night, while you sleep, a constant spray of neutrinos emanating from the sun comes up through your floor, passing through your bed and exiting through the roof toward the stars.

The production of neutrinos in the sun depends critically upon temperatures and pressures at its core. Because they do not interact with their surroundings, they pass easily to the surface and escape without restraint (unlike the photons of light we are presently receiving, which were generated about one million years ago, and were bounced about from atom to atom on their way from the center to the surface). Traveling at the speed of light, neutrinos complete the journey from the sun's core to the Earth's surface in approximately eight minutes. If we could detect and count them, their day-to-day numbers would tell us something about present rates of solar activity. But how does one go about detecting particles that will pass with impunity through any detector?

Fortunately for Earth-based experiments, if you have lots of neutrinos (and the sun provides us with *lots* of them—every second, more than 100 billion neutrinos are passing through the period at the end of this sentence), you don't have to throw a great deal of material in their path to cause a collision and capture one. Since 1970, a tank

Libertad

Shawnee

This mosaic of six *Viking Orbiter 1* photos shows the northeast portion of the Plain of Chryse. Each frame covers an area approximately 45 kilometers (28 miles) across. Meandering, intertwining channels flowing north (toward the top of the page) appear to have been cut by running water in Mars' geological past. *Reprinted through the courtesy of National Aeronautics and Space Administration, California Institute of Technology, Jet Propulsion Laboratories.*

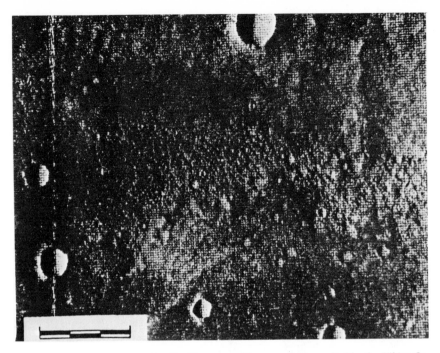

This region of possible near-surface liquid water on Mars was photographed by the *Viking Orbiter I* spacecraft. The region, known as an oasis of water vapor outgassing, is marked by several 10 kilometer (6.2 mile) wide craters and ancient lava flows. *Reprinted through the courtesy of National Aeronautics and Space Administration, California Institute of Technology, Jet Propulsion Laboratories.*

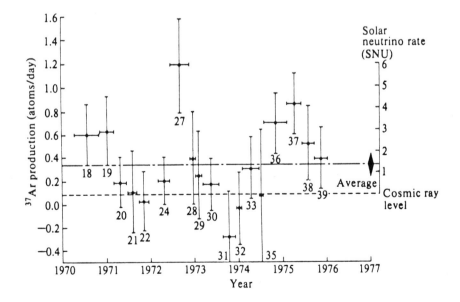

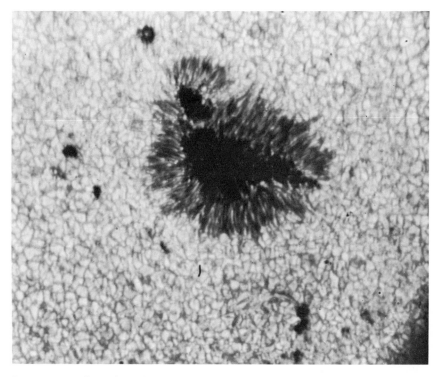

Sunspots are cool areas in the lower atmosphere of the sun. They occur in regions where power-ful magnetic lines bunch up in knots, producing temperatures about 2700°C cooler than the sur-rounding atmosphere. The granular areas outside the sunspot are convection currents on the sun's surface. This photograph is one of several thousand made from high-altitude balloons during Project Stratoscope, directed by Martin Schwarzschild of Princeton University.

containing 400,000 liters (approximately 100,000 gallons) of dry-cleaning fluid, a compound of chlorine, has been lying under 1500 meters (approximately one mile) of rock in a mineshaft in Colorado. A small number of the neutrinos passing through the tank interact with an isotope of chlorine (^{37}Cl) to produce argon atoms. Using very sensitive equipment, the few atoms of argon formed per week can be counted (the overlaying rock shelters the chlorine from cosmic rays, assuring researchers that only neutrinos are penetrating through to the

Results of experiments to detect solar neutrino production are shown as rates of detection of argon-37 atoms per day. The results suggest fluctuations that follow an approximately two-year cycle. © *Courtesy of the Astronomical Society of the Pacific.*

An old engraving (*top*) compared against a modern photograph shows the retreat of this mountain glacier since the end of the "Little Ice Age" approximately 300 years ago. *Courtesy of the National Center for Atmospheric Research/National Science Foundation.*

tank). The results obtained to date suggest fluctuations of energy output that seem to follow a two-year cycle.

We do not yet have a clear understanding of the sun's cycles. There are hints in the rings of very old trees that production of the radioactive isotope carbon-14 from the exposure of nitrogen-14 to cosmic rays in the upper atmosphere has varied in the past. Living and fossil trees record several anomalies in the history of atmospheric carbon-14 production over the last 7,000 years. One of these anomalies corresponds to a period from 1645 through 1715, during which sunspot activity was almost totally absent. This was a time of unusually severe winters in Europe and China, a time frequently referred to as the "Little Ice Age."

In those days there were not 3 billion, and more, human beings squeezed border against border from pole to pole. There were new resources for the taking, virgin continents to be explored: plenty of baskets in which to put one's eggs. If ice and drought did threaten a population, there were, in most parts of the world, sparsely inhabited places to move to; and men did not protect their territories with deuterium-tipped arrows. And so, it is with a sense of alarm that some astronomers have turned their attention to the sun and its neighbors on the other side of the sky. Their desire to learn more about the activity cycles of stars is no longer rooted in mere childlike curiosity.

13
Last Word

An object like Saturn's satellite Rhea, which appears as a minute speck in an earthly telescope, can be used to illustrate what the Voyagers *are expected to achieve. No surface features on Rhea have ever been seen. The photos from* Voyager 1 *will include images of Rhea displaying about 20 percent of its surface to nearly one-mile resolution—equivalent to the best Earth-based telescopic photographs of our own satellite, the moon.*

Dick Hoagland

A quick and infallible test of the imagination quotient of your friends and lovers. Quote the above; if s/he says, "So what?" or "What good is that?" ask for your ring back and walk away fast.

Harlan Ellison

The only solid piece of scientific truth about which I feel totally confident is that we are profoundly ignorant about nature. Indeed, I regard this as the major discovery of the past hundred years of biology. It is, in its way, an illuminating piece of news. It would have amazed the brightest minds of the eighteenth-century Englightenment to be told by any of us how little we know, and how bewildering seems the way ahead. It is this sudden confrontation with the depth and scope of ignorance that represents the most significant contribution of twentieth-century science to the human intellect.

Lewis Thomas

Passing into history now, gone almost beyond recall, is an age when the moon and Saturn's rings seemed very far away. We are the last generation of sapience upon this planet to have wondered what the

Sunset on Mars. *Reprinted through the courtesy of National Aeronautics and Space Administration, California Institute of Technology, Jet Propulsion Laboratories.*

surface of Mars or Rhea must look like. Those arriving after us will always know. The men and women who may one day settle the moon will already have a good idea what to expect. Airless skies have become commonplace.

When the first men stepped off the Earth, television screens were mounted in Grand Central Station and our minds were flooded with strange, new images. The world collectively held its breath. A few years later, when *Viking-1* landed on Mars, mankind breathed more easily. In New York, news-commentator David Hartman observed, "Where else but in the United States can you get up in the morning and watch live pictures coming from Mars?"

None of the science fiction writers had ever guessed what was about to happen. They had all been wrong.

Nobody knew what color the sky was on Mars. Nobody really knew what the rocks and soil would look like. For all we did know, a little black knot of Martians might have been advancing with a white flag.

Yet before even one-half of the television screen had become filled with our first glimpse of the red wilderness, *Good Morning America* went off the air to be replaced by scheduled reruns of *Magilla Gorilla* cartoons.

In 1980, we Americans spent 2.9 billion dollars on one of the space program's most celebrated spinoffs: *Space Invaders.* That is nearly one billion dollars more than was allocated to the space shuttle program during the same year. Meanwhile, a *Saturn 5* rocket, once built to carry men to the moon, lay on its side in Florida. A few pieces were missing, apparently taken for souvenirs. This sorry giant, when we met her early one morning, carried nothing more glamorous than the beer cans somebody had tossed into her engines. One side of her hull proclaimed that B.B. and J.M. were forever, and that John and Martha from Omaha had been there.

So what? What are rocks and outer space worth, anyway?

We have begun to know ourselves, that's what: through descents into stone and ascents into space.

But where can that possibly lead?

Perhaps nowhere; but we doubt it. No one could have predicted, when the Soviets threw that first ball of magnesium into the ionosphere, that we could, as a result, today possess a global network of satellite communications and pocket computers; or that tens of thousands of us would either be dead or wishing to be so were it not for post-*Mariner* image enhancers: the CAT (Computerized Axial Tomography or "brain scan"), and the still-evolving PET scan (this instrument is to an X-ray what a CAT is to a surgeon's probe: it literally permits the visualization of brains in action). There are more. We could add examples of spinoffs endlessly, each with crucial points in their development rooted in space research (sadly, we must list cruise missiles among these). The most remarkable thing about spinoffs is that they are almost always unanticipated by the very people who make them possible. Researchers, booming ahead into new territory, are bound to learn something new—even if, in doing so, they also succeed in demolishing the very hypotheses upon which their work is based. Surprises are emerging steadily from all quarters of science, passing around from mind to mind, and sometimes getting connected together in startling fashion.

But what if all the probing and discovering had not produced a single "useful" spinoff? Not a single one. What if the best thing we could say about close-up pictures of Saturnian rings was "Beautiful! Look at that!" followed by laughter? Would that be so bad? Is there something fundamentally hazardous or wasteful about learning for learning's sake alone?

Like creatures following some deeply placed instinct, we are driven to form for ourselves a simplified and lucid image of where we came from and, now that we are here, where we fit in with the rest of the universe. Certainly, we can get along without such knowledge; but the pursuit, almost every step of the way, has been a celebration of mystery and surprise.

The most beautiful emotion we can experience is the mysterious. Without it, Columbus, Darwin, and Armstrong would have stayed at home, we would not have the foggiest idea of how we got here or what stars are (nor would we care), and, it seems a good guess, there would never have been agriculture, electricity, the Beatles, Stravinski, or the anatomical drawings of Leonardo da Vinci. Looking around, it is nice to see that unsolved puzzles lie in every direction. We should be able to work our way to all of them, if we pay attention and if we are wise enough to avoid putting into practice the thermonuclear inverse to the golden rule.

Bibliography

Readers interested in further explanations of the topics covered in this book may find the following lists of publications helpful.

Bang!
Asimov, I., "The Very Large Lion and the Very Small Mouse," *Omni,* Vol. 3, pp. 78–83, 108; August, 1981.
Barrow, J.D. and Silk, J., "The Structure of the Early Universe," *Scientific American,* Vol. 242, pp. 118–129; April, 1980.
Bath, G.T. (Ed.), *The State of the Universe.* Oxford University Press, 1980.
Harrison, E.R., *Cosmology.* Cambridge University Press, 1981.
Overbye, D., "Messenger at the Gates of Time," *Science 81,* Vol. 2, pp. 60–67; June, 1981.
Silk, J., *The Big Bang.* W.H. Freeman and Co., 1980.
Waldrop, M.M., "Matter, Matter, Everywhere . . . ," *Science,* Vol. 2, pp. 803–806; February 20, 1981.
Weinberg, S., *The First Three Minutes.* Bantam Books, 1979.
Wilczek, F., "The Cosmic Asymmetry Between Matter and Antimatter," *Scientific American,* Vol. 243, pp. 82–90; December, 1980.

A Fall of Hydrogen
Einstein, A., *Relativity: The Special and General Theory.* Crown, 1931.
Frankel, T., *Gravitational Curvature: An Introduction to Einstein's Theory.* W.H. Freeman and Co., 1979.
Hawking, S. and Ellis, G., *The Large Scale Structure of Space-Time.* Cambridge University Press, 1973.
Jastrow, R., *Red Giants and White Dwarfs.* Warner Books, Inc., 1980.
Kaufman, W.J., *Astronomy: The Structure of the Universe.* Macmillan, 1977.
Misner, C., et al., *Gravitation.* W.H. Freeman and Co., 1973.
Sagan, C., *Cosmos.* Random House, 1980.
Silk, J., "Origin of the Galaxies," *Nature,* Vol. 292, pp. 409–411; July 30, 1981.

The Emergence of Carbon

Andrew, B.H., ed., *Interstellar Molecules.* Reidel, Boston, 1980.

Darwin, C., *The Origin of Species.* John Murry, 1859. (Mayr, E., ed., Facsimile Edition. Harvard University Press, 1964).

Davies, P., *Other Worlds.* Simon and Schuster, 1981.

Dickerson, R.E., and Geis, I., *Chemistry, Matter, and the Universe.* W.A. Benjamin, Inc., 1976.

Douglas, A.E., "Origin of Diffuse Interstellar Lines," *Nature,* Vol. 269, pp. 130–132; September 8, 1977.

Goldanskii, V.I., "Interstellar Grains as Possible Cold Seeds of Life," *Nature,* Vol. 269, pp. 583–584; October 13, 1977.

Hoyle, F., and Wickramasinghe, N.C., "Prebiotic Molecules and Interstellar Grain Clumps," *Nature,* Vol. 266, pp. 241–242; March 17, 1977.

Hoyle, F. and Wickramasinghe, N.C., *Life Cloud.* Sphere Books Ltd., 1978.

Macbeth, N., *Darwin Retired.* Dell Publishing Co., Inc., 1971.

McDonnell, J.A.M. (Ed.), *Cosmic Dust.* John Wiley and Sons, 1978.

Sagan, C., "Interstellar Organic Chemistry," *Nature,* Vol. 238, pp. 77–80; July 14, 1972.

Trefil, J.S., *From Atoms to Quarks.* Charles Scribner's Sons, 1980.

From Stardust

Anders, E. "Meteorites and the Early Solar System," *Annual Review of Astronomy and Astrophysics,* Vol. 9, pp. 1–34; 1971.

Batten, A.H., *Binary and Multiple Systems of Stars.* Pergamon Press, 1973.

Burnham, R., "Alpha Centauri." In *Burnham's Celestial Handbook,* Vol. 1. Dover Publications, Inc., 1978.

Grossman, L., "Condensation of the Primitive Solar Nebula," *Geochimica et Cosmochimica,* Vol. 36, pp. 597–619; May, 1972.

Grossman, L., and Larimer, J.W., "Early Chemical History of the Solar System," *Reviews of Geophysics and Space Physics,* Vol. 12, pp. 71–101; 1974.

Grossman, L., "The Most Primitive Objects in the Solar System," *Scientific American,* Vol. 232, pp. 30–38; February, 1975.

Herbst, W., and Assousa, G.E., "Supernovas and Star Formation," *Scientific American,* Vol. 241, pp. 138–145; August, 1979.

Schramm, D.N., and Clayton, R.N., "Did a Supernova Trigger the Formation of the Solar System?" *Scientific American,* pp. 98–113; October, 1978.

Shklovskii, I.S., *Stars: Their Birth, Life and Death.* W.H. Freeman and Co., 1978.

Touchstones

Bondy, S.C. and Harrington, M.E., "L-Amino Acids and D-Glucose Bind Stereo-specifically to a Colloidal Clay," *Science,* Vol. 203, March 23, 1979.

Claus, G., "Studies on Terrestrial Contaminants of Meteorites," *Annals of the New York Academy of Sciences,* Vol. 147, Art. 9, pp. 363–409; July 29, 1968.

Cronin, J.R. and Moore, C.B., "Amino Acid Analyses of the Murchison, Murray and Allende Carbonaceous Chondrites," *Science,* Vol. 172, pp. 1327–1329; June 25, 1975.

Cronin, J.R., et al., "Amino Acids in an Antarctic Carbonaceous Chondrite," *Science,* Vol. 206, pp. 335–337; October 19, 1979.

Gehrels, T. (Ed.), *Asteroids.* University of Arizona Press, 1979.

Hayatsu, R., et al., "Phenolic Ethers in the Organic Polymer of the Murchison Meteorite," *Science,* Vol. 207, pp. 1202–1204; March 14, 1980.

Janos, L., "Timekeepers of the Solar System," *Science 80,* Vol. 1, pp. 44–55; May, 1980.

Kerr, R.A., Isotopic Anomalies in Meteorities: Complications Multiply," *Science,* Vol. 202, pp. 203–204; October 13, 1978.

Lawless, J.G., et al., "Organic Matter in Meteorites," *Scientific American,* Vol. 226, pp. 38–46; June, 1972.

Lawless, J.G., "Amino Acids in the Murchison Meteorite," *Geochim Cosmochin Acta,* Vol. 37, No. 9, pp. 2207–2212; 1973.

Lee, T., et al., "Aluminum -26 in the Early Solar System: Fossil or Fuel?" *Astrophysical Journal,* Vol. 211, pp. L 107–L 110; 1977.

Marvin, U.B., "The Search for Antarctic Meteorites," *Sky and Telescope,* Vol. 62, pp. 423–427; 1981.

McCall, G.J., *Meteorites and Their Origins.* John Wiley and Sons, 1973.

METEORITE ISSUE (Special), *Natural History,* Vol. 90; April, 1981.

Nagy, B., et al., "Discussion of meteoritic Hydrocarbons and Extraterrestrial Life," *Annals of the New York Academy of Science,* Vol. 93, Art. 14, pp. 658–660, 663–664; 1962.

Nagy, B., et al., "Optical Activity in Saponified Organic Matter Isolated from the Interior of the Orgueil Meteorite," *Nature,* Vol. 202, pp. 228–233; 1964.

Nagy, B., *Carbonaceous Meteorites.* Elsevier, 1975.

Wetherill, G.W., "The Allende Meteorite," *Natural History,* pp. 102–107; September, 1978.

On Probability and Possibility

Buvet, R., and Ponnamperuma, C. (Eds.), *Molecular Evolution I: Chemical Evolution and the Origin of Life.* North-Holland, Amsterdam, 1971.

Cairns-Smith, A., "The Origin of Life and the Nature of the Primitive Gene," *The Journal of Theoretical Biology,* pp. 53–88; September, 1966.

Chedd, G., "Genetic Gibberish in the Code of Life," *Science 81,* Vol. 2, pp. 50–55; November, 1981.

Dickerson, R.E., "Chemical Evolution and the Origin of Life," *Scientific American,* Vol. 239, pp. 70–86; September, 1978.

Eigen, M., "Self-Organization of Matter and the Evolution of Biological Macromolecules," *Die Naturwissenshaften,* Vol. 59, pp. 465–532; October, 1971.

Eigen, M., et al., "The Origin of Genetic Information," *Scientific American,* Col. 244, pp. 88–118; April, 1981.

Folsome, C.E., *The Origin of Life: A Warm Little Pond.* W.H. Freeman and Co., 1979.

Fox, S.W., and Dose, K., *Molecular Evolution and the Origin of Life.* W.H. Freeman and Co., 1972.

Fox, S.W., "Origins of Biological Information and the Genetic Code," *Molecular and Cellular Biochemistry,* Vol. 3, pp. 129–142; 1974.

Gutfreund, H. (Ed.), *Biochemical Evolution.* Cambridge University Press, 1981.

Krammer, A., "Fueling the Third Reich," *Technology and Culture,* Vol. 19, p. 394; July, 1978.

Novick, R.P., "Plasmids," *Scientific American,* Vol. 243, pp. 102–127; December, 1980.

Wolfe, S.L., *Biology: The Foundations.* Wadsworth Publishing Co., 1977.

All This and Heaven Too?

American Geophysical Union, Washington D.C., *Scientific Results of the Viking Project;* September 30, 1977.

Folsome, C.E. and Brittain, A., "Model Protocells Photochemically Reduce Carbonate to Organic Carbon," *Nature,* Vol. 291, pp. 482–484; June 11, 1981.

Gore, R., "Sifting for Life in the Sands of Mars," *National Geographic;* January, 1977.

Gould, S.J., "The First Forebear," *Natural History,* Vol. 89, pp. 20–28; May, 1980.

Hodgson, G.W., and Baker, B.L., "Evidence for Porphyrins in the Orgueil Meteorite," *Nature,* Vol. 202, pp. 125–131; April 11, 1964.

Kerridge, J.F. and Macdougall, J.D., "Clues to the Origin of Sulfide Minerals in CI Chondrites," *Earth and Planetary Science Letters,* Vol. 43, No. 3, pp. 359–367; June, 1979.

Kerridge, J.F., et al., "Magnetite in CI Carbonaceous Meteorities: Origin by Aqueous Activity on a Planetismal Surface," *Science,* Vol. 205, pp. 395–397; July 27, 1979.

Klein, H.P., "The Viking Biological Investigations: Review and Status," *Origins of Life,* Vol. 9, pp. 157–160; 1979.

Morrowitz, H.J., *Energy Flow in Biology: Biological Organization as a Problem in Thermal Physics.* Academic Press, 1968.

Nagy, B., et al., "Organic Particles Embedded in Minerals in the Orgueil and Ivuna Carbonaceous Chondrites," *Nature,* Vol. 193, pp. 1129–1133; March 24, 1962.

Nagy, B., et al., "Electron Probe Microanalysis of Organized Elements in the Orgueil Meteorite," *Nature,* Vol. 198, pp. 121–125; 1963.

Nagy, B. (Ed.), "Life-like Forms in Meteorites and the Problems of Environmental Control on the Morphology of Fossil and Recent Protobionta," *Annals of the New York Academy of Sciences,* Vol. 108, Art. 2, pp. 339–616; June 29, 1963.

Nagy, B., et al., "Abiotic Graphitic Microstructures in Micaceous Metaquartzite about 3760 Million Years Old from Southwestern Greenland: Implications for Early Precambrian Microfossils," *Proceedings of the National Academy of Sciences,* Vol. 72, pp. 1206–1209; March 1975.

Pang, K.D., et al., "The Composition of Phobos: Evidence for Carbonaceous Chondrite Surface from Spectral Analysis," *Science,* Vol. 199, pp. 64–66; January 6, 1978.

Ponnamperuma, C., et al., "Possible Surface Reactions on Mars: Implications for Viking Biology Results," *Science,* Vol. 197, pp. 455–457; July 29, 1977.

Srinivasan, B. and Anders, E., "Noble Gases in the Murchison Meteorite: Possible Relics of s-Process Nucleosyuthesis," *Science,* Vol. 201, pp. 51–55; July, 1978.

Strick, M.R. and Barghoorn, E.S., "Extraterrestrial Abiogenic Organization of Organic Matter: The Hollow Spheres of the Orgueil Meteorite," *Space Life Sciences,* vol. 3, pp. 89–107; 1971.

Urey, H.C., "Biological Material in Meteorites: A Review," *Science,* Vol. 151, pp. 157–166; January 14, 1966.

Van Valen, L., "Energy and Evolution," *Evolutionary Theory,* Vol. 1, p. 179–229; 1976.

Ice

Beatty, J.K., "Voyager's Encore Performance," *Sky and Telescope,* Vol. 58, pp. 206–216; September, 1979.

Beatty, J.K., et al. (Eds.), *The New Solar System.* Sky Publishing Corp., 1981.

Berry, R., "Voyager: Science at Saturn," *Astronomy,* Vol. 9, pp. 6–22; February, 1981.

Felbeck, H., "Chemoautotrophic Potential of the Hydrothermal Vent Tube Worm, *Riftia pachyptila* Jones (Vestimentifera)," *Science,* Vol. 213, pp. 336–338; July 17, 1981.

Flaser, F.M., et al., "Titan's Atmosphere: Temperature and Dynamics," *Nature,* Vol. 292, pp. 693–698; August 20, 1981.

Gore, R., "What Voyager Saw: Jupiter's Dazzling Realm," *National Geographic,* Vol. 157, pp. 2–29; January, 1980. (Rick Gore is presently preparing an article on the planets, including Titan, for the Geographic.)

Hiatt, B., "Sulfides Instead of Sunlight," *Mosaic,* pp. 15–21; August, 1980.

Holger, W.J., and Wirsen, C.O., "Chemosynthetic Primary Production at East Pacific Sea Floor Spreading Centres," *Bioscience,* Vol. 29, pp. 592–598; October, 1979.

Morrison, D., "Four New Worlds," *Astronomy,* Vol. 8, pp. 6–22; September, 1980.

Parmentier, E.M., et al., "The Tectonics of Ganymede," *Nature,* Vol. 295, pp. 290–293, January 28, 1982.

Pollack, H.N., and Chapmann, D.S., "The Flow of Heat from the Earth's Interior," *Scientific American,* Vol. 237, pp. 60–67; August, 1977.

RISE Project Group, "East Pacific Hot Springs and Geophysical Experiments," *Science,* Vol. 207, pp. 1421–1433; March 28, 1980.

Soderblom, L.A., "The Galilean Moons of Jupiter," *Scientific American,* Vol. 242, pp. 88–100; January, 1980.

VOYAGER ISSUES (Special), *Science.* Vol. 204, June 1, 1979; Vol. 206, November 23, 1979; Vol. 212, April 10, 1981; Vol. 215, January 29, 1982.

Fire and Rain

Des Marias, D.J., et al., "Molecular Carbon Isotopic Evidence for the Origin of Geothermal Hydrocarbons," *Nature,* Vol. 292, pp. 826–828; August 27, 1981.

Folsome, C.E., et al., "Production of Hydrazines and Carbohydrazides in the Earth's Primitive Atmosphere," *Nature;* (in preparation).

French, B.M., "What's New on the Moon?" *Sky and Telescope,* Vol. 53, pp. 164–169, 258–261; March and April, 1977.

Gold, T. and Soter, S., "The Deep-Earth Gas Hypothesis," *Scientific American,* Vol. 242, pp. 154–161; June, 1980.

Goody, R.M. and Walker, J.C.G., *Atmospheres.* Prentice-Hall, 1972.

Hartmann, W.K., "The Moon's Early History," *Astronomy,* Vol. 4, pp. 6–16; September, 1976.

Kvenvolden, K. (Ed.), *Geochemistry and the Origin of Life,* Vol. 14. Academic Press, 1974.

McSween, H.Y. and Stolper, E.M., "Basaltic Meteorites," *Scientific American,* Vol. 242, pp. 54–63; June, 1980.

Ridley, W., "Petrology of Lunar Rocks and Implication to Lunar Evolution," *Annual Review of Earth and Planetary Sciences,* pp. 15–48; 1976.

Sebel, D. "Interview: Thomas Gold," *Omni,* pp. 85–86, 128–132; December, 1980.

Siever, R., "The Earth," *Scientific American,* Vol. 233, pp. 83–90; September, 1975.

Wasserburg, G.J., et al., "The Accumulation and Bulk Composition of the Moon," *Philosophical Transactions of the Royal Society of London,* A 285, pp. 7–22; 1977.

Woods, J.A., "The Moon," *Scientific American,* Vol. 233, pp. 93–102; September, 1975.

Punctuated What?

Associated Press Release (Los Angeles), "Fossil Turns Back Clock of Life," *Newsday,* page 3; June 20, 1980.

Eldredge, N., "Survivors from the Good Old, Old, Old Days," *Natural History,* Vol. 84, pp. 60–69; 1975.

Eldredge, N., "Alternative Approaches to Evolutionary Theory," *Bulletin of the Carnegie Museum of Natural History,* Vol. 13, pp. 7–19; 1979.

Fox, G.E., et al., "The Phylogeny of Prokaryotes," *Science,* Vol. 209, pp. 457–463; July 25, 1980.

Gould, S.J. and Eldredge, N., "Punctuated Equilibria: The Tempo and Mode of Evolution Reconsidered," *Paleobiology,* Vol. 3, pp. 115–151; 1977.

Gould, S.J., *Ever Since Darwin.* W.W. Norton and Co. Inc., 1977.

Gould, S.J., "A Darwinian Paradox," *Natural History,* Vol. 88, pp. 32–43; January, 1979.

Gould, S.J., "Is a New and General Theory of Evolution Emerging?" *Paleobiology,* Vol. 6, pp. 119–130; 1980.

Gould, S.J., "Hopeful Monsters," *Natural History,* Vol. 89, pp. 6–15; October, 1980.

Gould, S.J., "Hen's Teeth and Horse's Toes," *Natural History,* Vol. 89, pp. 24–28; July, 1980.

Johnston, R.F. and Selander, R.K., "House Sparrows: Rapid Evolution of Races in North America," *Science,* Vol. 144, pp. 548–550; 1964.

Lewin, R., "Evolutionary History Written in Globin Genes," *Science,* Vol. 214, pp. 426–429; October 23, 1981.

Lewin, R., "No Gap Here in the Fossil Record," *Science,* Vol. 214, pp. 645-646; November 6, 1981.

Malmgren, B.A. and Kennett, J.P., "Phyletic Gradualism in a Late Cenozoic Planktonic foraminiferal Lineage, *Paleobiology,* Vol. 7, pp. 156-166; 1981.

Newell, N.D., "Paleontological Gaps and Geochronology," *Journal of Paleontology,* Vol. 36, page 592; 1962.

Orpen, J.L. and Wilson, J.F., "Stromatolites at ≅ 3,500 Myr and a Greenstone-Granite Unconformity in the Zimbabwean Archaean," *Nature,* Vol. 291, pp. 218-220; May 21, 1981.

Pellegrino, C.R., "The Role of Desication Pressures and Surface Area/Volume Relationships on Seasonal Zonation and Size Distribution of Four Intertidal Decapod Crustacea From New Zealand: Implications for Adaptation to Land," *Comparative Biochemistry and Physiology;* In Press.

Schopf, J.W., and Oehler, D.Z., "How Old Are the Eucaryotes?" *Science,* Vol. 193, pp. 47-49; 1976.

Schopf, T.J.M. (Ed.), *Models in Paleobiology.* Freeman, Cooper, and Co., 1972.

Schopf, T.J.M., "Punctuated Equilibrium and Evolutionary Stasis," *Paleobiology,* Vol. 7, pp. 156-166; 1981.

Simpson, G.G., *The Major Features of Evolution.* Columbia University Press, 1953.

Stanley, S.M., *Macroevolution.* W.H. Freeman and Co., 1979.

Walter, M.R., et al., "Stromatolites 3,000-3,500 Myr Old from the North Pole Area, Western Australia," *Nature,* Vol. 284, pp. 443-445; April 13, 1980.

Ebb Tide

Alvarez, L., et al., "Extraterrestrial Cause for the Cretaceous-Tertiary Extinction," *Science,* Vol. 208, pp. 1095-1108; June 6, 1980.

Beals, C.S., "Fossil Meteorite Craters," *Scientific American,* Vol. 199, pp. 32-39; July, 1958.

Beatty, J.K., "Crater Hunting in Brazil," *Sky and Telescope,* Vol. 59, pp. 464-467; June, 1980.

Calame, O. and Mulholland, J.D., "Lunar Crater Giordano Bruno: A.D. 1178 Impact Observations Consistent With Laser Ranging Results," *Science,* Vol. 199, pp. 875-877; February 24, 1978.

Gould, S.J., "The Belt of an Asteroid," *Natural History;* August, 1980.

Hartmann, W.K., "Cratering in the Solar System," *Scientific American,* Vol. 236, No. 1, pp. 84-99; January, 1977.

Hickey, L.J., "Land Plant Evidence Compatible with Gradual, Not Catastrophic, Change at the End of the Cretaceous," *Nature,* Vol. 292, pp. 529-531; August 6, 1981.

Kent, D.V., et al., "Asteroid Extinction Hypothesis," *Science,* Vol. 211, pp. 648-656; February 13, 1981.

Kerr, R.A., "Asteroid Theory of Extinctions Strengthened," *Science,* Vol. 210, pp. 514-517; October 31, 1980.

Krinov, E.L., *Giant Meteorites.* Pergamon Press, Ltd., 1966.

Kyte, F.T., et al., "High Noble Metal Concentrations in a Late Pliocene Sediment," *Nature,* Vol. 292, pp. 417–420; July 30, 1981.

METEORITE ISSUE (Special), *Astronomy,* Vol. 9; April, 1981.

Margulis, L., *Symbiosis in Cell Evolution;* W.H. Freeman and Co., 1981.

Pellegrino, C.R., "Life in an Upper Cretaceous Sea," *Earth Science,* Vol. 31, pp. 53–57; April, 1978.

Rubin, A.E., "Glass Menagerie," *Griffith Observer,* Tectite Issue, pp. 2–9; April, 1979.

Smit, J. and Klaver, G., "Sanidine Spherules at the Cretaceous-Tertiary Boundary Indicate a Large Impact Event," *Nature,* Vol. 292, pp. 47–49; July 2, 1981.

Death Watch

Alexander, T., "Plate Tectonics Has a Lot to Tell Us about the Present and Future Earth," *Smithsonian,* Vol. 5, pp. 38–47; 1975.

Archibald, J.D., "The Earliest Known Paleocene Mammal Fauna and Its Implications for the Cretaceous-Tertiary Transition," *Nature,* Vol. 291, pp. 650–652; June 25, 1981.

Axelrod, D.I., "Origin of the Deciduous and Evergreen Habitats in Temperate Forests," *Evolution,* Vol. 20, pp. 1–15; 1966.

Axelrod, D.I. and Bailey, H.P., "Cretaceous Dinosaur Extinction," *Evolution,* Vol. 22, pp. 595–605; 1968.

Bakker, R.T., "Ecology of the Brontosaurs," *Nature,* Vol. 229, pp. 172–174; January 15, 1971.

Bakker, R.T., "Dinosaur Renaissance," *Scientific American,* Vol. 232, pp. 58–78; April, 1975.

Carey, F.G., "Fishes With Warm Bodies," *Scientific American;* February, 1973.

Case, G.R., *Pictorial Guide to Fossils.* Van Nostrand Reinhold Co., 1982.

Colbert, E.H., et al., "Temperature Tolerances of the American Alligator and Their Bearing on the Habits, Evolution, and Extinction of the Dinosaurs," *American Museum of Natural History Bulletin,* Vol. 86, pp. 327–374; 1946.

Darwin, C., *Journal of Researches into the Natural History and Geology of Countries Visited during the Voyage of the H.M.S. Beagle Round the World.* J. Murray, London, 1845.

Dicke, R.H., "Solar Luminosity and the Sunspot Cycle," *Nature;* July 5, 1979.

Eddy, J.A., "The Maunder Minimum," *Science;* June 18, 1976.

Eddy, J.A., "How Constant is the Sun?" *Natural History,* Vol. 88, pp. 80–88; December, 1979.

Emiliani, C., "Isotopic Paleotemperatures," *Science,* Vol. 154, pp. 851–856; 1966.

Gould, S.J., "Chance Riches," *Natural History,* Vol. 89, pp. 36–44; November, 1980.

Haxton, W.C. and Crowan, G.A., "Solar Neutrino Production of Long-Lived Isotopes and Secular Variations in the Sun," *Science,* Vol. 210, pp. 897–899; November 21, 1980.

Hickey, J.R., et al., "Initial Solar Irradiance Determinations from Nimbus 7 Cavity Radiometer Measurements," *Science,* Vol. 208, pp. 281–283; April 18, 1980.

Imbrie, J. and Imbrie, J.Z., "Modeling the Climatic Response to Orbital Variations," *Science,* Vol. 207, pp. 943–953; February 29, 1980.

Kukla, G., et al., "Orbital Signature of Interglacials," *Nature,* Vol. 290, pp. 295–300; March 26, 1981.

Langenheim, J.H., "Amber: A Botanical Inquiry," *Science,* Vol. 163, pp. 1157–1169; March 14, 1969.

Larkin, P.A. (Ed.) *The Investigations of Fish Power Problems.* Institute of Fisheries, University of British Columbia, 1958.

Larsson, S.G., "Baltic Amber: A Paleobiological Study," *Entomonograph,* Vol. 1. (Scandinavian Science Press Ltd., Klampenborg, Denmark); February 1, 1978.

Lowenstam, L.A. and Epstein, S., "Cretaceous Paleotemperatures as Determined by the Oxygen Isotope Method, Their Relations to and the Nature of Rudistid Reefs," *International Geological Congress, Symposium del Cretacio,* pp. 65–76; 1959.

Margolis, S.V. and Kennett, J.P., "Antarctic Glaciation during the Tertiary Recorded in Sub-Antarctic Deep-Sea Cores," *Science,* Vol. 170, pp. 1085–1088; 1970.

Narin, A.E.M. (Ed.), *Problems in Paleoclimatology.* Interscience Publication, 1964.

Newell, N.D., "Crises in the History of Life," *Scientific American,* Vol. 208, pp. 76–92; 1963.

Newell, N.D., "An Outline History of Tropical Organic Reefs," *American Museum Novitates,* No. 2465, pp. 1–37; September 21, 1971.

Overbye, D., "The Ghost Universe of Neutrinos," *Sky and Telescope,* Vol. 60, p. 115; August, 1980.

Parkinson, J.H., et al., "The Constancy of the Solar Diameter over the Past 250 Years," *Nature,* Vol. 288, pp. 548–551; December 11, 1980.

Pellegrino, C.R., "Vault of the Ages," *Smithsonian* (In Press).

Pieri, D.C., "Martian Valleys: Morphology, Distribution, Age, and Origin," *Science,* Vol. 210, pp. 895–897; November 21, 1980.

Rice, P.C., *Amber: The Golden Gem of the Ages.* Van Nostrand Reinhold Co., 1980.

Robock, A., "The Little Ice Age: Northern Hemisphere Average Observations and Model Calculations," *Science,* Vol. 206, pp. 1402–1404; 1980.

Sanders, H.L. and Hessler, R.R., "Ecology of the Deep Sea Benthos," *Science,* Vol. 163, pp. 1418–1424; 1969.

Schopf, T.J.M., "Permeo-Triassic Extinctions: Relation to Sea Floor Spreading," *The Journal of Geology,* Vol. 82, pp. 129–143; March, 1974.

Shapiro, I.I., "Is the Sun Shrinking?" *Science,* Vol. 208, pp. 51–53; April 4, 1980.

Stevens, G.R., *New Zealand Adrift.* A.H. and A.W. Reed, Ltd., 1980.

Stuiver, M., and Quay, P.D., "Changes in Atmospheric Carbon-14 Attributed to a Variable Sun," *Science,* Vol. 207, pp. 11–20; January 4, 1980.

Thunell, R.C., "Cenozoic Paleotemperature Changes and Planktonic Foraminiferal Speciation," *Nature,* Vol. 289, p. 670–672; February 19, 1981.

Whalley, P. and Jarzembowski, E.A., "A New Assessment of Rhyniella, the Earliest Known Insect from the Devonian of Rhynie, Scotland," *Nature,* Vol. 291, p. 317; May 28, 1981.

Williams, G.E., "Sunspot Periods in the Late Precambrian Glacial Climate and Solar-Planetary Relations," *Nature,* Vol. 291, pp. 624–628; June 25, 1981.

Wilson, O.C., et al., "The Activity Cycles of Stars," *Scientific American,* Vol. 244, pp. 104–119; February, 1981.

Zisk, S.H., and Mouginis-Mark, P.J., "Anomalous Region on Mars: Implications for Near-Surface Liquid Water," *Nature,* Vol. 288, pp. 735–738; December 18, 1980.

Index

Page entries in italics refer to captions and footnotes.